DIFFERENTLY

THINKING

AI Native Government

A Blueprint for Reimaging Government for the Digital Era

Mohammad J. Sear

"Visionaries imagine and create new realities by challenging and disregarding the status quo..."

Mohammad J. Sear

First Edition

Author: Mohammad J. Sear

Editor & Design: Publishing Spot:

Publisher: Mohammad J. Sear

ISBNs:

- E-book: 978-969-8692-78-0
- Paperback: 978-969-8692-79-7
- Hardcover: 978-969-8692-80-3

Author's Website: https://mjmsear.com/

Printed in USA

Table of Contents

PREFACE

I believe Artificial Intelligence (AI), and particularly generative AI and agentic AI are the biggest disrupters of the digital era that we are living in today, and this book which has been developed by extensively leveraging these technologies is a living proof of this disruption.

The primary objective of this book is to equip government officials, leaders and public sector professionals with the necessary understanding of AI, its capabilities and potential, and the associated risks on the one hand and provide insights and frameworks that will enable them to effectively benefit from the power of AI.

As technology continues to evolve at an unprecedented pace, governments must adapt to leverage AI's potential for enhancing service delivery, improving decision-making, and fostering transparency. This book aims to provide a comprehensive understanding of how AI can be utilized to create a more efficient, responsive, and citizen-centric government.

Another critical objective is to explore the ethical implications and governance challenges associated with the adoption of AI in public administration. As governments increasingly rely on data-driven methodologies, it is imperative to address concerns surrounding privacy, bias, and accountability. This book seeks to engage readers in a thoughtful discourse on establishing robust ethical frameworks that ensure AI technologies are implemented responsibly and equitably. By doing so, it aims to promote a culture of trust between the government and the citizens it serves.

The book also intends to highlight best practices and successful case studies of AI implementation in various public sector contexts. By showcasing examples from around the world, readers will gain insights into practical applications of AI that have led to enhanced operational efficiency and improved public outcomes. These case studies will serve as a valuable resource for policymakers and practitioners, offering tangible strategies that can be adapted to their unique organizational environments.

Furthermore, this book aims to stimulate critical thinking about the future landscape of government in the context of AI advancements. It encourages readers to envision a proactive approach where government agencies not only adapt to technological changes but also anticipate future trends and challenges, and more importantly look to reimagine themselves for the AI era. By fostering a forward-thinking mindset, the book seeks to inspire leaders within government and the public sector to innovate continuously and cultivate a culture of agility and resilience.

Lastly, the "AI Native Government" book aspires to bridge the gap between academia and practice by providing a foundational understanding of AI technologies, coupled with actionable insights for government officials, leaders and public sector professionals. It also serves as a resource for educators and consultants, who are striving to guide and advise on how to harness the transformative power of AI. By aligning theoretical knowledge with practical applications, this book endeavors to catalyze a new era of government that is inherently AI-native, ultimately leading to improved governance and enhanced citizen engagement in the digital age.

About the Author

Mohammad J. Sear is a digital era futurist and thought leader, and is focused on bringing purpose to the benefits of the digital era for nations. He likes to think of himself as a Chief Disruption Officer.

He has obtained leadership training from the Harvard Kennedy School of Government, USA and holds an MBA from the University of Leicester, UK.

He is the author of the book "Becoming Digital Nations – reimagining countries for the digital era".

After a successful 12+ years career in the UK government during the premiership of Margaret Thatcher, John Major and Tony Blair Mohammad moved to the private sector and has now for 20+ years been advising government, public and private sector organizations in the UK, Middle East,

Africa, Australasia and South Asia on strategic challenges and digital transformation.

He is currently leading the Digital Government & Public Sector and Start-up practices across the Middle East and North Africa for a global consultancy firm, and in the past for a 3 year period he was also a Digital Government, Public Sector and Innovation lecturer at the Paris School of International Affairs, Sciences Po, France.

He is a catalytic public sector changemaker and champion of diversity & inclusion, and passionate about transforming government. Being a change agent with a bias towards action he has enabled governments to become more citizen-centric and achieve operational breakthroughs by harnessing conventional and digital capabilities, as well as leveraging the power of design thinking, agile, behavioral science, emerging technologies such as artificial intelligence.

He is sought after by senior leaders' in government, public and private sectors for his futuristic and strategic thinking, and surgical advisory capabilities.

As a thought-leader and author of publications in the areas of digital nations, society, economy and governance, citizen centricity, customer experience, service design & delivery, emerging technologies Mohammad is frequently requested to speak, moderate or be a panel member at top tier global events on topics including but not limited to: digital nations, emerging technologies, future of governance, humanizing technology, exponential digital transformation in countries, cross sector collaboration, citizen-centered governance, and design thinking in public policy.

Some of the articles he has authored include:

> Digital is great but exclusion isn't – make data work for driving better digital inclusion published in Harvard Business Review

> Holistic Digital Government published in the MIT Technology Review

> Want To Make Citizens Happy - Put Experience First published in Forbes Middle East

And others such as "Bringing Purpose to Digital in Government", "How Digital is Changing the Way We Listen to Customers", "How Can GCC Governments Sustainably Deliver Better Citizen Experiences", "What is the Cure for a Better Patient Experience in the GCC", "Application of the Global Star Rating System for Public Services".

Moving from insights to execution Mohammad has designed transformational initiatives in several areas such as GovTech and Innovation Labs, digital product accelerators, digital government transformation, digital government service models and national citizen experience measurement strategies.

Chapter 1:

Introduction: Defining the AI Native Government

Beyond E-Government and Digital Government: The Shift from AI Adoption to AI Native

The evolution of government interaction with technology has progressed through distinct phases, from basic digitization, e-government and digital government initiatives focused on improving service delivery efficiency [1] to the current era where Artificial Intelligence (AI) presents transformative potential. However, much of the current AI deployment within the public sector represents 'AI adoption' – integrating AI tools into existing structures and processes, often in a piecemeal or experimental fashion.[3] This approach, while potentially beneficial for specific tasks, falls short of realizing AI's full capacity to reshape government.

The concept of "AI Native Government" signifies a more profound transformation. It moves beyond merely using AI as an add-on tool towards a state where AI is intrinsic to the government's very architecture – influencing its design, deployment, operation, and maintenance.[5] An AI Native Government leverages a pervasive, data-driven, and knowledge-based ecosystem where AI capabilities are naturally embedded within functionalities and/or the function is completely reimagined to deliver its designated mandate . This involves augmenting or replacing static, rule-based mechanisms with learning and adaptive AI systems where appropriate.[5] This represents a fundamental architectural and operational shift, moving beyond the digitization of existing services towards the creation of intelligent, adaptive systems capable of continuous learning and improvement.[6]

This systemic integration and/or reimagining distinguishes the AI Native approach from previous e-government and digital government phases.[7] Early government AI experiments often focused on automating specific tasks or improving efficiency within existing silos.[3] In contrast, becoming AI Native requires a cohesive, "whole-of-government" strategy [7] that integrates AI across functions or reimagines the functions themselves. It necessitates rethinking processes, structures, and the very nature of government, supported by integrated data infrastructure [9], unified data platforms [11], and comprehensive governance frameworks.[12] This integrated/reimagined system, conceptualized as an "Algorithmic State Architecture," forms the core of the AI Native paradigm [6], marking a significant departure from simply applying AI tools to legacy systems.

Core Principles and Characteristics of an AI Native Government

An AI Native Government is not defined solely by its technological sophistication but by its adherence to a core set of principles and its operational characteristics. These principles, drawn from established AI ethics and governance frameworks, are not merely guidelines but fundamental design requirements, crucial for ensuring legitimacy, public trust, and responsible innovation in an era of algorithmic decision-making.[1] The high stakes involved in government AI applications, which directly impact citizens' rights and access to essential services [3], demand a values-driven approach.

Key principles underpinning the AI Native Government include:

8

- **Alignment with Human Values and Societal Expectations:** AI systems must be designed and operated in ways that align with democratic values, ethical standards, and societal goals, ensuring they contribute positively to human objectives without causing unintended harm.[12]

- **Robustness, Security, and Safety:** AI systems must be reliable, stable, predictable, and secure throughout their lifecycle, functioning appropriately under various conditions and resilient against errors, misuse, or adversarial attacks.[13] Mechanisms for override, repair, or decommissioning in case of failure or harm are essential.[18]

- **Transparency and Explainability:** There must be clarity and openness regarding how AI systems operate, the data they use, and the logic behind their decisions, fostering understanding, trust, and the ability to audit or challenge outcomes.[12]

- **Fairness, Equity, and Non-discrimination:** AI systems must be designed and deployed to avoid perpetuating or amplifying biases, ensuring equitable treatment and outcomes for all individuals and groups, consistent with civil rights protections.[13]

- **Accountability:** Clear mechanisms must exist to assign responsibility for the development, deployment, and outcomes of AI systems, enabling redress for harms and ensuring oversight.[16]

- **Privacy and Data Protection:** The collection, use, and retention of data, particularly personal data, must adhere to strict privacy principles and legal regulations, safeguarding individual rights.[13]

- **Human-Centeredness and Oversight:** AI should augment human capabilities and be subject to appropriate human judgment and oversight, especially in decisions with significant consequences for individuals' rights or well-being.[17]

- **Respect for Law and Human Rights:** AI deployment must fully comply with applicable laws, respect human dignity, and uphold fundamental rights and freedoms.[12]

Beyond these principles, the characteristics of an AI Native system, adapted from frameworks developed in other sectors [5], provide an operational lens:

- **Purpose:** AI implementations are mission-driven, designed to achieve specific, often complex, governmental objectives where data-driven approaches offer significant advantages over traditional methods.

- **Environment:** AI systems possess awareness of their operational context, capable of detecting and adapting to variations in data sources, infrastructure, or regulatory landscapes.

- **Intelligence:** Systems exhibit the ability to learn, adapt, and evolve by integrating new data and observations, continuously improving their performance and strategies to meet objectives.

- **System:** Encompasses the entire lifecycle management of AI functionality, ensuring trustworthiness, fairness, explainability, safety, and control, while enabling interaction and data sharing within a broader ecosystem.

- **Outcome:** Focused on delivering tangible value, such as enhanced public services, autonomous actions based on derived insights, and enabling future AI-centric government architectures.

Embedding these principles and characteristics into the technical and operational fabric of government is the central challenge and defining feature of the AI Native government.

Goals: Efficiency, Enhanced Services, Data-Driven Policy, Public Trust

The transition towards an AI Native Government is driven by a set of ambitious goals aimed at fundamentally transforming public administration and its relationship with citizens. These goals represent a potential leap beyond incremental improvements, targeting systemic changes in how a government operates and delivers value.

1. **Radical Efficiency and Cost Savings:** A primary driver is the potential for AI and automation to dramatically improve operational efficiency, streamline bureaucratic processes, and reduce costs.[3] Automating repetitive tasks, optimizing workflows, and improving resource allocation can free up significant human and financial resources, particularly crucial in contexts of budget constraints.[21] Estimates suggest substantial productivity gains are possible through AI adoption in the public sector.[21]

2. **Enhanced Public Services and Citizen Experience:** Governments aim to leverage AI to meet rising citizen expectations, often shaped by experiences with the private sector [21], by delivering higher quality, more accessible, personalized, and responsive public services.[1] This includes using AI for 24/7 citizen support via chatbots [29], tailoring services to individual needs [21], and simplifying interactions with government agencies.[8]

3. **Data-Driven and Predictive Policy Making:** AI offers the capability to move beyond reactive or intuition-based policy towards evidence-based, predictive, and potentially simulated approaches.[3] Analyzing vast datasets can identify emerging trends, forecast needs, model the potential impacts of different policy options, optimize resource allocation, and evaluate program effectiveness with greater sophistication.[3]

4. **Strengthened National Security and Competitiveness:** For many nations, adopting AI is seen as crucial for maintaining national security, enhancing defense capabilities, countering adversaries who are also leveraging AI, and ensuring economic competitiveness in a global landscape increasingly shaped by technological prowess.[1]

5. **Building and Maintaining Public Trust:** Underpinning all other goals is the objective of fostering and sustaining public trust.[1] This involves demonstrating that AI is being used responsibly, ethically, transparently, and effectively for the public good, addressing concerns about bias, privacy, and accountability proactively.[12]

Achieving these goals requires navigating inherent tensions. The drive for efficiency must be balanced against the need for fairness and equity; personalization must respect privacy; data-driven insights must be transparent and contestable. Therefore, robust governance is not just a constraint but an essential enabler for realizing the transformative potential of AI Native Government in a sustainable and legitimate manner.[12]

The Imperative for Transformation: Why AI Native is Necessary

The transition to an AI Native model is increasingly framed not merely as an opportunity for improvement but as a necessary adaptation for governments to remain effective, relevant, and resilient in the 21st century.

Several converging factors create this imperative:

- **Pace of Technological Change and Geopolitical Competition:** AI is an era-defining technology [20] advancing at an unprecedented rate.[46] Governments risk strategic disadvantage, both economically and in terms of national security, if they fail to keep pace with AI developments and adoption by other nations or potential adversaries.[20] Leading in responsible AI development and application is seen as crucial for maintaining influence and security.[13]

- **Rising Citizen Expectations:** Citizens, accustomed to the seamless, personalized digital experiences offered by the private sector, increasingly expect similar levels of service quality, speed, and responsiveness from government.[21] Failure to modernize and meet these expectations risks eroding public satisfaction and trust.[21]

- **Increasing Complexity of Societal Challenges:** Governments face increasingly complex, interconnected, and rapidly evolving challenges, such as climate change, pandemics, cybersecurity threats, demographic shifts, and global economic volatility.[3] Addressing these effectively requires sophisticated analytical, predictive, and simulation capabilities that often exceed traditional methods but can be enhanced by AI.[3]

- **Fiscal Pressures and the Need for Efficiency:** Many governments operate under significant budget constraints while facing growing demands for public services.[21] AI offers the potential for substantial productivity improvements, cost savings through automation, and optimized resource allocation, making it an attractive tool for enhancing state capacity within fiscal limits.[21]

- **Proactive Risk Management:** The widespread proliferation of AI technologies itself creates new risks and potential societal disruptions, including job displacement, bias amplification, privacy infringements, and the spread of misinformation.[13] Governments have a responsibility to understand and proactively manage these risks, which requires developing internal AI expertise and governance capacity – essentially, becoming more AI-native themselves to govern AI effectively.[12]

Inaction or merely incremental adoption is increasingly seen as a perilous course.[21] Governments that fail to strategically integrate AI risk becoming less effective, less competitive, less trusted, and less capable of addressing the challenges and opportunities of the AI era. The imperative is therefore not just to use AI, but to fundamentally integrate its capabilities and principles into the core functioning of the government[6] or to reimagine its functioning all together for this AI era we are living in today.

Chapter 2

Foundational Pillars: Technology and Data Infrastructure

The Data Imperative: Strategy, Governance, Quality, and Security

Data serves as the fundamental substrate upon which AI Native Government is built. Without a strategic, well-governed, high-quality, and secure data foundation, AI initiatives are prone to failure, inaccuracy, bias, and erosion of public trust.49 Recognizing data as a critical strategic asset, rather than a mere byproduct of operations, is paramount. This necessitates a comprehensive approach encompassing several key dimensions:

- **Data Strategy:** Government agencies must move beyond ad-hoc data usage to develop a clear, overarching strategy.[9] This involves identifying critical data assets, defining how data will support specific government missions and AI use cases, establishing priorities for data collection and enhancement, and creating pathways for responsible data sharing and access across silos.[9] Identifying authoritative data sources and ensuring datasets are "AI-ready" – meaning they are suitable for training and deploying AI models – is a core component.[9] Leadership, potentially through a dedicated Chief Data Officer (CDO), is crucial for driving this strategy.[53]

- **Data Governance:** A robust data governance framework is essential to manage data assets effectively and ethically throughout their lifecycle.[12] This includes establishing clear policies for data creation, storage, access, usage, sharing, retention, and deletion.[56] It requires defining roles and responsibilities (e.g., data stewards, governance boards [54]), implementing data cataloging and metadata management 9, and ensuring compliance with legal and regulatory requirements, such as privacy laws like GDPR and CCPA.[56] Frameworks like the NIST AI RMF incorporate data governance as a key component.[67]

- **Data Quality:** The maxim "garbage in, garbage out" is acutely relevant for AI.[49] Poor data quality – including inaccuracies, incompleteness, inconsistencies, outdatedness, and inherent biases – is a primary reason for AI project failures and can lead to unreliable, unfair, or harmful outcomes.[41] Achieving AI readiness requires significant investment in data quality management processes, including data cleansing, validation, standardization, normalization, enrichment, and ongoing monitoring.[56] Tackling data quality issues often necessitates addressing underlying problems in legacy systems and breaking down data silos.[69] Innovative techniques like synthetic data generation may offer partial solutions for specific challenges like privacy preservation or augmenting limited datasets, but require careful validation.[70]

- **Data Security and Privacy:** Government agencies handle vast amounts of sensitive citizen and operational data, making security and privacy paramount.[73] Robust security measures, including encryption, strict access controls (e.g., Role-Based Access Control - RBAC, Multi-Factor

Authentication - MFA), continuous monitoring for breaches or anomalies, and secure data storage and transmission protocols, are non-negotiable.[56] Privacy-preserving techniques (e.g., anonymization, pseudonymization, differential privacy) should be employed where appropriate.[63] Compliance with data protection regulations is essential not only legally but also for maintaining public trust.[57]

The transition to an AI Native data paradigm requires substantial organizational change, dedicated resources, and sustained leadership commitment. Neglecting the data foundation significantly increases the risk of AI initiatives failing to deliver value or, worse, causing harm.[50] The data imperative underscores that successful AI Native Government is as much about effective data management as it is about sophisticated algorithms.

Building the Engine: AI Infrastructure Requirements (Cloud, Compute/GPU, Edge)

An AI Native Government requires a modern, flexible, and powerful technological infrastructure capable of supporting diverse and demanding AI workloads. This infrastructure is typically a hybrid ecosystem combining different components, strategically deployed to meet specific needs for scalability, performance, real-time processing, and security.[55] Key infrastructure requirements include:

- **Cloud Platforms:** Cloud computing (including public, private, hybrid, and specialized government clouds like AWS GovCloud [76] and Azure Government [78]) provides the essential foundation for scalability, flexibility, and access to a wide range of AI services and tools.[76] Cloud platforms allow government agencies to provision resources on

17

demand, manage costs more effectively (pay-as-you-go models), and leverage pre-built AI capabilities offered by major providers (e.g., Google Cloud AI [82], AWS Bedrock [80], Azure OpenAI Service [80]). For government use, adherence to security and compliance standards like FedRAMP (Federal Risk and Authorization Management Program) is critical for cloud service adoption.[76] The shift to cloud is often a prerequisite for large-scale AI deployment, enabling government agencies to overcome limitations of legacy on-premises systems.[55]

- **Compute Resources (HPC/GPUs):** Training sophisticated AI models, particularly deep learning algorithms and large language models (LLMs), is computationally intensive and demands specialized hardware.[84] High-Performance Computing (HPC) clusters and, most notably, Graphics Processing Units (GPUs) are essential for accelerating these tasks.[84] Access to sufficient GPU capacity (e.g., from NVIDIA [85], AMD [86]) is a critical bottleneck for many AI initiatives. This necessitates investment in either on-premises GPU farms, cloud-based GPU instances [80], or hybrid approaches. Furthermore, the deployment of high-density AI hardware requires considerations for data center infrastructure, including advanced power delivery and cooling solutions to manage the significant energy consumption and heat generation.[55]

- **Edge Computing:** Not all AI processing can or should happen in centralized data centers or the cloud. Edge computing brings computation and data storage closer to the sources of data generation or where AI decisions need to be acted upon in real-time.[55] This is crucial for applications requiring low latency (e.g., autonomous systems, real-time surveillance analysis), operating in

18

environments with limited connectivity (e.g., tactical military settings), or handling highly sensitive data that should not leave a specific location.55 Government use cases include public safety monitoring [94], traffic management optimization [94], infrastructure monitoring 95, and supporting military operations at the tactical edge.[92] An effective edge strategy requires seamless integration and data flow between edge devices and central systems.[55]

- **Networking:** A robust, high-bandwidth, and low-latency network infrastructure is the connective tissue of the AI Native ecosystem. It is essential for transferring large datasets between storage, compute resources (cloud, HPC, edge), and end-users; enabling real-time data streams for analysis and inference; and supporting distributed AI systems.[55] Technologies like 5G play an increasingly important role, particularly in enabling advanced edge computing applications and supporting mobile or IoT-based AI deployments.[92]

Architecting this infrastructure requires careful planning, considering the specific needs of different AI use cases (e.g., training vs. inference), data sensitivity levels, latency requirements, and budget constraints. It represents a significant shift from traditional, often siloed, government IT infrastructure towards a more integrated, flexible, and powerful platform designed for the demands of the AI era.[90]

The AI Toolkit: Understanding Key Technologies (ML, NLP, CV, GenAI) in Government Context

An AI Native Government leverages a diverse portfolio of AI technologies, each with distinct capabilities suited to different public sector challenges. Understanding the core functions, applications, benefits, and limitations of these key technologies is crucial for strategic deployment.

- **Machine Learning (ML):** This foundational AI capability involves algorithms learning patterns and making predictions or decisions from data without being explicitly programmed for every scenario.[8] In government, ML is widely applied for:

  - *Prediction & Forecasting:* Identifying crime hotspots (predictive policing) [36], forecasting disease outbreaks [35], predicting demand for public services [3], anticipating infrastructure maintenance needs [29], and modeling economic trends.[39]

  - *Detection:* Identifying fraudulent transactions or applications [37], detecting anomalies in network traffic for cybersecurity [106], or spotting unusual patterns in health data.[35]

  - *Optimization:* Improving resource allocation based on predicted needs.[3]

- **Natural Language Processing (NLP):** NLP equips machines with the ability to understand, interpret, and generate human language (text and speech).[28] Key government applications include:

  - *Citizen Interaction:* Powering chatbots and virtual assistants to answer queries, provide information, and guide users through processes.[8]

  - *Information Processing:* Analyzing and summarizing large volumes of text, such as public comments on regulations [107], citizen feedback [28], policy documents [109], or intelligence reports.[109]

  - *Communication:* Facilitating translation services [109] and improving accessibility.[112]

- *Monitoring:* Identifying trends, sentiment, or misinformation in social media and online forums.[28]

- **Computer Vision (CV):** CV enables machines to "see" and interpret information from images and videos.[28] Government use cases are expanding rapidly:

  - *Public Safety & Security:* Facial recognition for identifying suspects or missing persons [99], analyzing surveillance footage for anomaly detection or threat identification [114], and border security monitoring.[114]

  - *Infrastructure & Environment:* Monitoring traffic flow [114], inspecting infrastructure (roads, bridges) for defects [114], analyzing satellite imagery for environmental changes or agricultural monitoring.[35]

  - *Administration:* Digitizing documents through Optical Character Recognition (OCR) and Handwritten Text Recognition (HTR).[8]

- **Generative AI (GenAI):** A subset of AI focused on creating novel content, including text, images, code, and synthetic data.[8] Emerging government applications include:

  - *Content Creation:* Drafting reports, summaries, emails, press releases, and other communications.[28]

  - *Coding & Modernization:* Assisting developers in writing, debugging, and modernizing code, potentially bridging legacy systems.[28]

  - *Enhanced Interaction:* Powering more sophisticated and conversational chatbots and virtual assistants.[28]

  - *Simulation & Analysis:* Creating synthetic data for training other AI models or simulating policy scenarios.[34]

- *Personalization:* Developing personalized learning materials or citizen communications.[121]

- **Agentic AI:** A subset of AI that goes beyond traditional automation and even generative AI by empowering systems to act autonomously, make decisions, and achieve predefined goals with minimal human oversight. Emerging government applications include:

  - *Autonomous Process Management:* Streamlining complex administrative workflows, such as permit approvals or grant disbursements, with intelligent, self-executing systems.

  - *Proactive Public Services:* Deploying AI agents to monitor public infrastructure for issues, anticipate citizen needs, and initiate interventions (e.g. dispatching maintenance crews before a system fails).

  - *Intelligent Data Analysis & Policy Implementation:* Utilizing agents to continuously analyze vast datasets for policy insights, identify compliance gaps, and even autonomously execute policy adjustments or alerts.

  - *Enhanced Cybersecurity & Threat Response:* Automating threat detection, analysis, and immediate response actions to cyberattacks, significantly reducing human response times.

  - *Personalized Citizen Engagement & Support:* Providing highly personalized and proactive support by agents that understand individual citizen needs and can navigate various government services on their behalf.

The following table summarizes these key technologies and their relevance:

AI Technology	Core Capability	Example Government Use Cases	Potential Benefits	Key Challenges/ Risks
Machine Learning (ML)	Learning patterns, prediction, classification	Predictive policing [97], fraud detection [103], demand forecasting [3], resource optimization [36], health risk prediction [35]	Improved efficiency, proactive interventions, better resource allocation, data-driven insights	Data quality dependency, bias amplification [72], lack of explainability ("black box"), potential for errors in predictions
Natural Language Processing (NLP)	Understanding & generating human language	Chatbots/virtual assistants [8], analyzing public feedback [28], document summarization /analysis [8], translation [111], misinformation detection [107]	Enhanced citizen engagement, improved accessibility, streamlined information processing, better understanding of public sentiment	Nuance/context misunderstanding, potential for biased language generation, handling diverse languages/dialects, data privacy in text analysis
Computer Vision (CV)	Interpreting visual information	Public safety surveillance [113], facial recognition [99], traffic analysis [114], infrastructure inspection [120], OCR/document digitization [8], environmental monitoring [117]	Improved situational awareness, enhanced security, automated inspection, efficient data capture	Privacy concerns (surveillance) [116], accuracy issues (esp. facial recognition bias [99]), high data storage/processing needs

23

Generative AI (GenAI)	Creating novel content (text, code, images)	Report/communication drafting [108], code generation/modernization [28], advanced chatbots [28], policy simulation [34], personalized training [121]	Increased productivity, accelerated development, enhanced creativity, improved user interaction	Hallucinations/inaccuracies [95], potential for misuse (deepfakes, disinformation) [125], data privacy risks, IP issues [125], bias generation
Agentic AI	Autonomous action, decision-making, and goal achievement with minimal human oversight. Systems perceive, reason, plan, and execute to achieve defined objectives.	Automated workflow management (e.g., permit approvals, grant disbursements), proactive public service delivery (e.g., predictive infrastructure maintenance, anticipating citizen needs), intelligent data analysis for policy implementation, autonomous cybersecurity threat response, and personalized citizen support.	Significant efficiency gains, cost savings, enhanced responsiveness in public services, improved decision-making through continuous data analysis, and increased operational resilience.	Ensuring accountability and transparency in autonomous decisions, managing ethical considerations and potential bias, addressing security vulnerabilities in autonomous systems, establishing clear governance frameworks, and navigating the complexity of integration with existing government infrastructure.

Successfully implementing AI Native Government involves selecting the appropriate tools from this toolkit based on the specific problem, data availability, ethical considerations, and desired outcomes, often requiring a combination of these technologies working in concert within an integrated architecture.

Architecting the Algorithmic State: Integrated Data Platforms and Systems

Transitioning to an AI Native Government necessitates a fundamental shift in how technological systems and data are architected. Isolated AI applications or siloed data repositories are insufficient; realizing the full potential requires an integrated, interoperable, and data-centric architectural approach.[5] This involves moving towards a cohesive system where infrastructure, data, algorithms, and services work in concert.

Key architectural concepts include:

- **Algorithmic State Architecture (ASA):** This conceptual framework provides a valuable lens for understanding the structure of an AI-enabled government.[6] It consists of four interdependent layers:

  1. *Foundational Layer (Digital Public Infrastructure - DPI):* Encompasses core infrastructure like cloud platforms, data centers, secure networks, identity management, and data exchange systems – the essential plumbing.[6]

  2. *Intelligence Layer (Data-for-Policy - DfP):* Focuses on the collection, processing, analysis, and governance of data to generate insights for policy and operations.[6] This layer relies heavily on the foundational DPI.

  3. *Process Layer (Algorithmic Government/Governance - AG):* Integrates AI and algorithms into core government processes for automation, prediction, optimization, and decision support, while embedding governance and

maintaining human oversight.[6] This layer consumes insights from the DfP layer.

4. *Service Layer (GovTech):* Represents the interface with citizens and other stakeholders, delivering AI-powered public services and applications built upon the underlying layers.[6] The ASA framework highlights that the effectiveness of higher layers (like GovTech services) is critically dependent on the robustness and maturity of the foundational layers (DPI, DfP).[11] Strategic coordination across these layers is essential.

- **Integrated Data Platforms:** Breaking down traditional data silos is crucial.[9] AI Native architectures often rely on integrated data platforms – such as Data Access Platforms (DAPs) [9] or Data Intelligence Platforms [10] – that provide a unified environment for data storage (e.g., data lakes, lakehouses [10]), governance, processing, analytics, and AI/ML model development and deployment.[10] These platforms facilitate secure data sharing and ensure AI models have consistent access to governed, high-quality data.[9] Architectures like Disaggregated, Shared-Everything (DASE) aim to overcome limitations of older systems for AI-scale data handling.[96]

- **AI-Centric Design and MLOps:** An AI Native architecture treats AI not as an add-on but as a core component from the outset.[5] This includes incorporating principles and practices for managing the entire lifecycle of AI models (Model Lifecycle Management or MLOps), covering development, training, deployment, monitoring, and retraining, ensuring models remain accurate, reliable, and governed over time.[5]

- **Interoperability and Open Standards:** To enable seamless integration and data flow across different systems, government agencies, and potentially external partners, interoperability is key.[11] This involves adopting open standards, utilizing Application Programming Interfaces (APIs) for data exchange [11], and designing systems with modularity and compatibility in mind.[11] Avoiding vendor lock-in through proprietary technologies is also a critical consideration.[131]

Building this integrated architecture requires significant strategic planning, investment, and often, modernization of legacy systems. It represents a move away from fragmented IT landscapes towards a unified, intelligent digital infrastructure capable of supporting the complex demands of an AI Native Government.

Chapter 3

AI in Action: Transforming Public Sector Functions

Enhancing Public Safety and Law Enforcement

The application of AI in public safety and law enforcement presents some of the most potent opportunities and complex ethical challenges for an AI Native Government. AI tools offer the potential to significantly enhance the efficiency and effectiveness of crime prevention, investigation, and response, but require careful governance to mitigate risks of bias and overreach.

Key applications include:

- **Predictive Policing:** Utilizing ML algorithms to analyze historical crime data, location information, and other factors to identify potential crime hotspots and forecast criminal activity.[36] The goal is to enable more effective resource allocation, deploying officers proactively to areas where crime is deemed more likely.[36] While some reports suggest effectiveness in reducing crime rates [134], significant concerns exist regarding the potential for these systems, often trained on historically biased data, to reinforce and amplify existing biases, leading to over-policing of certain communities.[44]

- **Identity Recognition:** AI, particularly computer vision, powers facial recognition and other biometric identification technologies used to identify suspects from surveillance footage, match fingerprints or DNA, and locate missing persons.[29] These tools can accelerate investigations.[115] However, accuracy issues, particularly concerning demographic variations (e.g., higher error rates for darker-skinned individuals [99]), raise serious fairness and civil liberties concerns.[99]

- **Surveillance and Anomaly Detection:** AI analyzes vast amounts of data from CCTV cameras, drones, sensors, and online sources to monitor public spaces, detect unusual or suspicious activities, track movements, and identify potential threats in real-time.[39] This enhances situational awareness but fuels concerns about mass surveillance and privacy infringement.[45]

- **Investigative Support:** AI assists investigators by analyzing evidence (e.g., 3D crime scene reconstruction, bullet trajectory analysis, DNA analysis [99]), processing large volumes of digital evidence (e.g., identifying child exploitation material online [119]), and uncovering links between cases.[8] NLP can also analyze witness statements or reports.[107]

- **Administrative Efficiency:** AI tools, including NLP, can automate the time-consuming process of writing police incident reports by transcribing audio from body cameras and generating initial drafts, freeing up officer time.[99] AI can also streamline other administrative tasks.[115]

- **Emergency Response:** AI can optimize the coordination and allocation of resources during emergencies by analyzing real-time data (e.g., [911] calls, social media, weather) [39] and predicting needs.

The deployment of AI in law enforcement necessitates stringent safeguards. The potential for AI systems to inherit and scale biases present in historical data is a major concern.[73] Transparency about how these tools are used, mechanisms for accountability when errors occur, and continuous auditing for fairness and accuracy are critical for maintaining public trust and ensuring compliance with legal and ethical standards.[99] The goal should be to use AI as a tool to augment human officers and investigators, improving their effectiveness while upholding civil rights and liberties.[115]

Revolutionizing Public Service Delivery and Citizen Experience

A core promise of AI Native Government is the transformation of how citizens interact with public services, moving away from often cumbersome, impersonal, and inefficient processes towards experiences that are more responsive, personalized, and accessible.[21] This shift aims to meet rising citizen expectations, largely influenced by the convenience and personalization offered by the private sector.[21]

Key AI applications driving this revolution include:

- **Intelligent Virtual Assistants and Chatbots:** AI-powered chatbots are increasingly deployed across government websites and platforms to provide 24/7 support, answer frequently asked questions instantly, guide citizens through complex application processes (e.g., benefits, licenses, loans), and triage inquiries, reducing wait times and call center workloads.[8] Examples include Singapore's "Ask Jamie" [29], the US Department of Education's "Aidan" [97], and USCIS's chatbot.[93] Generative AI enhances these tools, enabling more natural conversations and sophisticated responses.[28]

- **Personalized Service Delivery:** By analyzing citizen data (while respecting privacy), AI can enable governments to offer more tailored information, recommendations, and services.[21] This could involve proactively suggesting relevant benefits, providing personalized guidance based on individual circumstances, or customizing communication channels and formats.[21] Cities like Christchurch are exploring single digital identities and AI-driven recommendations.[30]

- **Streamlined Application Processing:** AI and automation can significantly speed up and simplify the processing of applications for benefits, permits, licenses, grants, and other government services.[8] This includes automating data entry (using OCR/HTR 8), verifying information, checking eligibility using ML [8], and managing workflows.[28]

- **Improved Accessibility:** AI can enhance accessibility through features like real-time translation for non-native speakers [29], simplifying complex government language [112], and providing information through multiple channels accessible to people with disabilities.[1]

- **Enhanced Citizen Engagement and Feedback Analysis:** AI tools can analyze public feedback from various sources like social media, surveys, and direct communications to gauge public sentiment, identify emerging issues, and inform service improvements.[28] This allows governments to be more responsive to citizen needs and concerns.

Case studies from jurisdictions like Singapore [29], Estonia [31], and various US agencies and cities [30] demonstrate tangible benefits, such as reduced workloads, faster response times, and improved citizen satisfaction.[29]

However, realizing this vision requires addressing significant challenges. Data integration across agency silos is often necessary for personalization and streamlined processing.[9] Ensuring equitable access and avoiding the creation of a new digital divide based on AI literacy or access is crucial.[48] Privacy concerns associated with collecting and analyzing citizen data for personalization must be meticulously managed through robust governance and transparency.[33] Critically, the goal is often to augment human service delivery, using AI to handle routine tasks while preserving human empathy, judgment, and intervention for complex or sensitive interactions.[8]

Optimizing Resource Allocation and Budgeting

In an environment often characterized by fiscal constraints and increasing service demands [26], AI offers government agencies powerful tools to optimize the allocation of limited resources and improve budgeting processes. By leveraging data analytics and predictive capabilities, AI can help ensure that public funds and personnel are deployed more efficiently and effectively, aligning spending with strategic priorities and citizen needs.[26]

Key applications include:

- **Predictive Demand Forecasting:** AI algorithms can analyze historical data, demographic trends, economic indicators, and other factors to forecast future demand for public services such as education enrollment, healthcare utilization, social assistance programs, infrastructure usage, and emergency services[3] These predictions allow agencies to plan resource needs proactively, avoiding shortages or over-allocation.[3]

- **Optimized Deployment of Assets and Personnel:** Based on predictive insights or real-time data analysis, AI can optimize the deployment of resources. Examples include dynamically allocating police patrols to predicted crime hotspots [36], directing emergency responders to areas of greatest need during disasters [39], scheduling infrastructure maintenance based on predicted failure rates [100], or optimizing public transit routes and schedules.[97]

- **AI-Driven Budgeting:** Moving beyond traditional line-item budgeting, AI tools can assist in the budgeting process itself.[26] They can analyze historical spending patterns across programs, identify potential efficiencies and cost savings, model the financial implications of different allocation scenarios, and help align budget decisions more closely with stated community priorities and program outcomes.[26] This supports a shift towards priority-based or performance-based budgeting.[26]

- **Procurement Optimization:** AI can enhance government procurement by forecasting demand for goods and services, analyzing vendor performance and risk, detecting anomalies in bids or contracts, streamlining review processes, and optimizing contract management.[28] This can lead to cost savings and more effective acquisition outcomes.[108]

Case studies, such as predicting hospital admissions to optimize resource planning [147] or using AI to guide grant allocations to areas of greatest need [105], illustrate the potential impact.

However, several challenges must be addressed. The effectiveness of these AI tools hinges critically on the availability of high-quality, comprehensive, and unbiased data.[49] Integrating data across different agencies or systems remains a significant hurdle.[148] Furthermore, the initial investment required for AI technologies, infrastructure, and skilled personnel can be substantial, posing a challenge for agencies facing tight budgets.[148] Overcoming these requires strategic investment, robust data governance, and demonstrating clear return on investment to justify expenditures.[152] The goal is to transition from reactive, often inefficient resource allocation practices to a proactive, data-informed, and optimized approach that maximizes public value.

Data-Driven Policy Making: Analysis, Simulation, and Forecasting

AI technologies hold the potential to significantly enhance the entire public policy lifecycle, making it more evidence-based, forward-looking, and responsive to complex societal dynamics.[3] By processing vast amounts of diverse data and employing sophisticated analytical techniques, AI can provide policymakers with deeper insights and more powerful tools for decision-making.[39]

Applications across the policy cycle include:

- **Agenda Setting and Problem Identification:** AI can analyze diverse data streams – including social media trends, citizen feedback, news reports, economic indicators, public health records, and environmental sensor data – to identify emerging public concerns, detect anomalies, understand public sentiment, and pinpoint policy needs often faster or more comprehensively than traditional methods.[28] For example, analyzing historical triage data helped identify public health risks in Victoria, Australia.[35]

- **Policy Formulation and Analysis:** AI can support the design of more effective policies. Predictive models can forecast the likely impacts (economic, social, environmental) of different policy options, allowing for comparison and refinement before implementation.[3] AI can simulate complex systems (e.g., economies, transportation networks, climate systems) to test policy interventions under various scenarios.[34] AI tools can also assist in evidence synthesis by rapidly summarizing relevant research literature or identifying inconsistencies in existing legislation.[34] Examples include using ML to assess tax policy impacts [35] or forecast the effects of green spending.[35]

- **Targeting and Implementation:** AI can help ensure policies are better targeted by identifying specific populations or geographic areas most in need or likely to be affected. Techniques like using computer vision on satellite imagery to map poverty enable more precise resource allocation for development programs.[35]

- **Policy Evaluation and Monitoring:** AI-powered analytics can provide more nuanced and timely evaluations of policy effectiveness by analyzing outcome data across various metrics and identifying causal relationships.[35] Real-time monitoring of data can also allow for adaptive policy adjustments.[38]

- **Regulatory Compliance:** AI can assist regulators by automating the monitoring of compliance with regulations, analyzing large volumes of submissions or transaction data to detect violations or anomalies.[39]

While the potential is significant, realizing data-driven policymaking with AI requires addressing key challenges. The quality, representativeness, and potential biases of the data used are critical concerns, as flawed data can lead to flawed policy insights.[34] The inherent complexity and potential opacity ("black box" nature) of some AI models can make it difficult to explain the rationale behind AI-informed policy recommendations, potentially undermining transparency and public accountability.[155] Effective use requires not only technical tools but also policymakers and analysts skilled in interpreting AI outputs critically and integrating them with domain expertise and ethical considerations. The aim is to augment human judgment in the policy process, not replace it entirely.[34]

Streamlining Administrative Efficiency: Automation (RPA) and Back-Office Functions

Beyond high-profile applications in public safety or citizen services, AI and related automation technologies like Robotic Process Automation (RPA) offer significant potential to improve the efficiency and effectiveness of internal government operations and back-office functions.[22] These applications often provide tangible and relatively quick returns on investment by tackling repetitive, high-volume administrative tasks.[22]

Key areas for automation include:

- **Automating Routine Tasks:** RPA excels at automating rule-based, repetitive tasks previously performed by humans.[22] This includes data entry, copying information between systems, generating standard reports, processing forms, and verifying documents.[8] AI capabilities like Optical Character Recognition (OCR) and Handwritten Text Recognition (HTR) can digitize paper documents or images, feeding data into automated workflows.[8]

- **Intelligent Process Automation:** Combining RPA with AI capabilities allows for the automation of more complex processes that involve some level of interpretation or decision-making. Examples include claims processing (e.g., welfare benefits, disability claims [147]), grant management [28], tax processing [22], and aspects of procurement.[28] AI can help classify documents, extract relevant information, check for compliance, or flag anomalies for human review.[28]

- **Compliance and Reporting:** AI and automation can assist in monitoring compliance with regulations and automating the generation of required reports, ensuring accuracy and timeliness while reducing manual effort.[22] Maintaining clean audit trails is another benefit.[22]

- **Workflow Optimization:** By automating steps and reducing manual handoffs, these technologies can streamline internal workflows, eliminate bottlenecks, and reduce overall processing times.[23]

- **Knowledge Management:** AI tools can help organize and search internal documents, policies, and knowledge bases, making information more accessible to government employees.[95]

Numerous case studies demonstrate significant benefits. The US IRS, DoD, and VA have reported substantial cost savings and processing time reductions through RPA implementation.[149] HHS agencies use AI to streamline grant management and risk assessment.[158] These efficiency gains are crucial for reducing administrative burden, minimizing errors [22], cutting operational costs [22], and, importantly, freeing up public servants to focus on more complex, strategic, or citizen-facing tasks that require human judgment and empathy.[25]

Successful implementation requires careful selection of processes suitable for automation (highly repetitive, rule-based, involving structured data are ideal for RPA [149]), clear understanding of the workflow [149], ensuring data quality, and managing integration with existing (often legacy) systems.[23] While RPA focuses on automating tasks, AI brings cognitive capabilities; their integration offers powerful potential for intelligent automation.[8] For many agencies, automating back-office functions represents a pragmatic and high-impact starting point on their AI journey.

Chapter 4

Governing the AI Native Government: Ethics, Accountability, and Trust

Establishing Robust AI Governance Frameworks

The transition to an AI Native Government, where AI is deeply embedded in operations and decision-making, necessitates the establishment of robust, comprehensive, and adaptive governance frameworks.[12] These frameworks are crucial not only for mitigating the inherent risks of AI – such as bias, privacy violations, security threats, and lack of transparency – but also for fostering innovation responsibly and building the public trust essential for legitimacy.[12] Governance cannot be an afterthought; it must be integrated into the design, development, deployment, and ongoing monitoring of AI systems.[159]

Governments can adopt different levels of governance maturity, ranging from informal approaches based on organizational values to ad-hoc policies developed in response to specific risks, and ultimately to formal, comprehensive frameworks.[12] Given the potential impact of government AI, a formal approach is generally required, involving structured policies, clear guidelines, defined roles and responsibilities (such as Chief AI Officers [14] and AI ethics boards [12]), risk assessment processes, ethical reviews, and oversight mechanisms.[12]

Several existing frameworks provide valuable guidance, although none may be sufficient alone for the unique public sector context. Key references include:

- **OECD AI Principles:** Adopted by over [40] countries [18], these principles offer a high-level, values-based foundation for trustworthy AI, emphasizing inclusive growth, human rights, transparency, robustness, and accountability.[18] They also provide policy recommendations for governments.[18] While influential globally [163], they require translation into specific operational guidelines.

- **NIST AI Risk Management Framework (RMF):** A voluntary framework developed in the US [159], the AI RMF provides a structured process for managing AI risks based on four core functions: Govern, Map, Measure, and Manage.[67] It aims to cultivate a risk management culture and offers practical guidance for identifying, assessing, and responding to AI risks throughout the lifecycle.[67] It is widely used as a reference, even outside the US.[165]

- **EU AI Act:** This landmark regulation adopts a risk-based approach, categorizing AI systems based on their potential for harm and imposing stricter requirements (including prohibitions for unacceptable risks) on higher-risk applications.[12] It mandates specific governance practices, risk management systems, data governance, transparency, human oversight, and conformity assessments for high-risk AI, with substantial financial penalties for non-compliance.[12]

- **US Executive Orders and OMB Guidance:** Recent US administrations have issued executive orders (e.g., EO 13960 1, EO 14110 [13], EO 14179 [166]) and subsequent Office of Management and Budget (OMB) memoranda (e.g., M-25-21 42) directing federal agencies on responsible AI use and

40

procurement. These mandate actions like appointing Chief AI Officers, establishing AI governance bodies, maintaining AI use case inventories, implementing minimum risk management practices for high-impact AI, and ensuring ethical considerations like privacy and civil rights are addressed.[13]

- Other Frameworks: Sector-specific guidelines (e.g., for intelligence [17], finance [12]) or general data ethics frameworks (e.g., GSA 170) also provide relevant principles.

Effective public sector AI governance likely requires synthesizing elements from these diverse sources, creating a tailored framework that aligns with national values, legal contexts, and specific government agency mission. This framework must be dynamic, capable of adapting to rapid technological advancements and evolving societal expectations.[56] It should move beyond compliance checklists to foster a genuine culture of responsible AI innovation.[67]

The following table provides a high-level comparison of some major frameworks:

Framework	Origin/ Scope	Key Principles/ Focus Areas	Approach	Key Requirements for Public Sector	Enforcement/ Penalties
OECD AI Principles	International (47 Adherents [19])	Values: Inclusive growth, human rights, transparency, robustness, accountability.[18] Policy Recommendations.	Values-based, Non-binding Principles	Guidance for national policies & international cooperation on R&D, ecosystem, governance, skills, cooperation.[18]	None directly

NIST AI RMF	US (Voluntary)	Risk Management (Govern, Map, Measure, Manage).[67] Trustworthiness Characteristics (valid, safe, secure, fair, etc.).[165]	Voluntary, Risk Management Process	Provides methodology for agencies to manage AI risks; supports compliance with US policies.[67]	None directly
EU AI Act	European Union (Binding Regulation)	Risk-based categorization (unacceptable, high, limited, minimal).[59] Requirements for high-risk AI (data, transparency, oversight, etc.).[12]	Regulatory, Risk-Based, Binding	Strict compliance required for AI systems deployed or used in the EU, including by public authorities. Specific obligations for high-risk systems (e.g., law enforcement, benefits).[12]	Significant fines for non-compliance.[12]
US EOs / OMB Memos	US Federal Agencies (Binding Directives)	Innovation, Governance, Public Trust, Risk Management, Procurement.[131] Specific safeguards for high-impact AI.[42]	Directive-based, Pro-innovation focus	Mandates CAIOs, inventories, risk assessments, specific procurement practices, training, transparency for federal agencies.[42]	Internal agency accountability

Core Ethical Principles: Transparency, Explainability (XAI), Fairness, Privacy, Security

At the heart of responsible AI governance lie core ethical principles that must guide the design, deployment, and use of AI systems in the public sector. These principles are not merely abstract ideals but have concrete implications for system architecture, data handling, algorithmic design, and human oversight.

- **Transparency and Explainability (XAI):** Transparency requires openness about how AI systems function, the data they consume, and the decisions they produce.[12] This is crucial for building trust and enabling accountability.[155] However, many advanced AI models, particularly deep learning systems, operate as "black boxes," making their internal reasoning difficult to decipher.[45] Explainable AI (XAI) encompasses techniques aimed at making these processes understandable to humans.[155] This involves providing clear justifications for specific outputs, tracing decisions back to input data, documenting the model's logic and limitations, and quantifying uncertainty.[155] Government applications, especially those impacting rights or safety, demand high levels of explainability to allow for scrutiny, challenge, and compliance verification.[63]

- **Fairness and Non-discrimination:** AI systems must be designed and evaluated to ensure they do not produce unfairly biased or discriminatory outcomes against individuals or groups, particularly based on protected characteristics like race, gender, or age.[13] This requires proactively identifying and mitigating biases that can arise from training data, algorithmic design, or deployment context.[175] Fairness is context-dependent, and achieving it often involves trade-offs with other objectives like accuracy.[174] Regular fairness audits and adherence to non-discrimination laws are essential.[175]

- **Privacy and Data Protection:** Given AI's reliance on data, protecting privacy is fundamental.[13] This involves adhering to data protection regulations (like GDPR [62] and CCPA [62]), implementing principles like data minimization (collecting only necessary data), purpose limitation (using data only for specified, legitimate purposes), ensuring data security, and respecting individual rights (e.g., access, correction, deletion, consent).[62] Privacy-enhancing technologies (PETs) may also play a role.[67]

- **Robustness, Security, and Safety:** AI systems must be dependable, perform consistently as expected, and be resilient to errors, failures, or malicious attacks.[13] This includes ensuring cybersecurity of the AI models and the infrastructure they run on [179], testing for vulnerabilities, and designing systems that fail safely or can be overridden if they pose unreasonable risks.[18]

- **Human-Centeredness, Autonomy, and Oversight:** AI should serve human goals and augment human capabilities, not replace human judgment inappropriately.[17] Systems must respect human dignity and autonomy.[17] Crucially, appropriate levels of human oversight and intervention must be maintained, particularly for high-impact decisions affecting individuals' rights, safety, or access to essential services.[17] The goal is collaboration between humans and machines, leveraging the strengths of both.[41]

Operationalizing these principles requires integrating them into every stage of the AI lifecycle, from initial conception and data collection through development, deployment, and ongoing monitoring. It often involves navigating complex trade-offs and requires continuous dialogue among technologists, policymakers, ethicists, and the public.[12]

Mitigating Bias and Ensuring Fairness in Algorithmic Systems

Algorithmic bias represents one of the most significant ethical challenges in deploying AI, particularly within the public sector where decisions can have profound impacts on individuals' lives and opportunities.[15] AI systems are not inherently objective; they learn from data, and if that data reflects historical or societal biases, the AI system is likely to learn, replicate, and potentially amplify those biases.[13]

Sources and types of bias are varied:

- **Data Bias:** Training data may underrepresent certain demographic groups (sampling bias [136]), contain inaccurate labels (label bias [178]), or reflect historical discrimination (historical bias [178]). Examples include facial recognition systems performing poorly on darker-skinned women due to unrepresentative training data [50] or predictive policing algorithms reflecting biased arrest patterns.[73]

- **Algorithmic Bias:** Bias can be introduced through the model design itself, such as choices about features, objective functions, or assumptions made by developers.[136] Algorithms might incorrectly infer causation from correlation or prioritize certain outcomes over others in ways that lead to unfairness.[72]

- **Human Bias:** Developers' own conscious or unconscious biases can influence system design and interpretation of results.[136] Bias can also enter during data annotation or when users interact with the system.[182]

The consequences of biased AI in government can be severe, leading to discriminatory outcomes in hiring [44], lending [44], criminal justice (e.g., risk assessments, sentencing) [41], healthcare access [178], and the allocation of social benefits.[41] This not only harms individuals but erodes public trust and undermines the legitimacy of government actions.[73]

Mitigating bias requires a proactive and multi-pronged strategy implemented throughout the AI lifecycle:

- **Data Diversity and Quality:** Conscious efforts must be made to collect diverse, representative datasets and address imbalances.[177] Data cleansing and preprocessing are crucial.[61]

Keeping sensitive attributes (like race or gender) in datasets during development allows for explicit bias testing.[178]

- **Fairness-Aware Algorithm Design:** Incorporating fairness metrics and constraints directly into the algorithm design and training process can help optimize for equitable outcomes.[177] Various technical approaches exist, though defining "fairness" itself is complex and context-specific.[174]

- **Bias Detection and Auditing:** Regularly testing and auditing AI systems specifically for bias using dedicated tools (e.g., Google's What-If Tool [185], Aequitas [185], Amazon SageMaker Clarify [185]) is essential both pre-deployment and post-deployment.[176] This includes evaluating performance across different demographic subgroups.[185]

- **Transparency and Documentation:** Clearly documenting data sources, model design choices, potential bias risks identified, and mitigation steps taken is crucial for accountability.[177]

- **Diverse Teams:** Involving diverse perspectives (across demographics, disciplines like ethics and social science) in the development and oversight process helps identify potential biases that might otherwise be overlooked.[136]

- **Ongoing Monitoring:** Bias can emerge or drift over time as data distributions change or models are updated. Continuous monitoring of deployed systems for fairness metrics is necessary.[177]

Addressing AI bias is an ongoing challenge that requires a combination of technical solutions, robust governance processes, diverse human oversight, and a commitment to ethical principles. It is fundamental to ensuring AI serves the public good equitably.

Algorithmic Accountability: Mechanisms, Challenges, and Case Studies (e.g., SyRI)

Accountability is a cornerstone of democratic governance, ensuring that public actors can be held responsible for their decisions and actions.[156] The increasing use of algorithms and AI systems in government decision-making introduces significant challenges to traditional accountability mechanisms.[156] Issues like the "black box" nature of complex algorithms (making it hard to understand why a decision was made) [155] and the diffusion of responsibility among developers, deployers, and human overseers can create an "accountability gap".[16]

Algorithmic accountability refers to the set of mechanisms designed to ensure that AI systems used in the public sector, and the human actors involved, can be held responsible for their operations and outcomes.[16] It requires the ability to explain and justify AI-driven actions and to impose consequences for failures or harms.[156]

A range of policy interventions and mechanisms are being explored and implemented to foster algorithmic accountability [187]:

- **Impact Assessments:** Requiring formal assessments (e.g., AI Impact Assessments, Data Protection Impact Assessments) before deploying AI systems, especially high-risk ones, to proactively identify and mitigate potential harms related to fairness, privacy, safety, and rights.[42] US OMB guidance mandates AI impact assessments for high-impact federal AI.[42]

- **Audits and Regulatory Inspection:** Conducting internal or independent third-party audits of AI systems to verify compliance with policies, assess performance, check for bias, and ensure technical robustness.[174]

- **Public Transparency:** Increasing public visibility into how government uses AI through mechanisms like public AI use case inventories [1], registries of algorithms, and clear communication about AI deployment.[186] Transparency allows for public scrutiny and holds agencies accountable.[186]

- **External/Independent Oversight Bodies:** Establishing dedicated bodies (e.g., AI ethics committees, ombudspersons, specialized regulators) with the authority and expertise to oversee AI development and deployment, investigate complaints, and enforce standards.[12]

- **Individual Rights and Redress:** Guaranteeing rights for individuals affected by AI decisions, including the right to an explanation, the right to human review of automated decisions, and the right to appeal or seek redress for erroneous or unfair outcomes.[42]

- **Procurement and Vendor Accountability:** Embedding accountability requirements into procurement processes, demanding transparency, testing capabilities, and clear documentation from vendors supplying AI systems to the government.[42]

Case studies provide crucial lessons. The Dutch SyRI (System Risk Indication) case, where an algorithmic system used to detect welfare fraud was challenged in court and ultimately found to violate human rights due to lack of transparency and potential bias, highlights the critical role of judicial review and civil society advocacy in enforcing accountability when internal mechanisms fail.[41] It underscores that technical complexity cannot absolve the state of its accountability obligations.[184] Similarly, studies of algorithms used in US child welfare [183] or education [183] reveal potential harms and the need for better evaluation and transparency.

Achieving effective algorithmic accountability requires a multi-layered approach combining technical solutions, procedural safeguards (like impact assessments and appeals), institutional oversight, and legal frameworks. It is an ongoing process, essential for ensuring AI serves democratic values.

Building and Maintaining Public Trust in AI Government

Public trust is the currency of legitimate governance, and it is particularly critical—and potentially fragile—in the context of AI Native Government.[1] Given the transformative power of AI, its inherent complexities, and documented instances of failure or misuse [41], citizens may harbor significant skepticism or fear regarding its use by the government.[41] Building and maintaining public trust is therefore not an optional extra but a prerequisite for the successful and sustainable adoption of AI in government.[25]

Trust is influenced by public perceptions of government competence, benevolence, and integrity in using AI. Key factors include [1]:

- **Perceived Fairness and Equity:** Belief that AI systems are not biased and treat all citizens equitably.

- **Transparency and Understanding:** Confidence that citizens can understand (at an appropriate level) how AI is being used and why decisions are made.

- **Security and Privacy:** Assurance that personal data is protected and AI systems are secure from misuse.

- **Reliability and Effectiveness:** Evidence that AI systems work correctly and deliver tangible benefits.

- **Accountability and Redress:** Knowledge that mechanisms exist to hold systems and decision-makers accountable and to rectify errors or harms.

- **Ethical Alignment:** Belief that AI use aligns with societal values and ethical principles.

Strategies for actively building and maintaining public trust include:

- **Proactive Transparency and Communication:** Governments must be open about where, why, and how they are using AI. This includes publishing use case inventories [169], providing clear explanations of AI systems in plain language [155], communicating limitations and risks alongside benefits [12], and avoiding hype.[190]

- **Meaningful Public Engagement:** Involving citizens, civil society groups, and diverse stakeholders in the dialogue around AI governance, development priorities, and ethical guidelines is crucial.[1] This fosters co-ownership and ensures AI development aligns with public values.

- **Demonstrating Ethical Governance:** Implementing and visibly adhering to robust ethical principles and governance frameworks signals a commitment to responsible AI use.[1] This includes conducting ethical impact assessments and ensuring human oversight.[42]

- **Ensuring Technical Robustness:** Demonstrating that AI systems are reliable, secure, and safe through rigorous testing, validation, and ongoing monitoring builds confidence in their technical competence.[13]

- **Providing Recourse Mechanisms:** Establishing clear channels for citizens to question, appeal, or seek redress for

AI-driven decisions they believe are unfair or incorrect is vital for accountability and trust.[42]

- **Highlighting Public Value:** Clearly communicating the tangible benefits that AI delivers for citizens – such as improved services, faster responses, or enhanced safety – helps build support and demonstrate the value proposition.[43]

- **Addressing Concerns Directly:** Acknowledging public concerns and skepticism about AI [41] and addressing them proactively through open dialogue and demonstrable safeguards is more effective than ignoring them.

Building trust is an ongoing effort requiring sustained commitment across all aspects of AI implementation. High-profile failures can quickly erode public confidence [41], making proactive risk management, ethical diligence, and transparent communication essential from the very beginning of the AI Native journey.

Cybersecurity Risks and Mitigation Strategies for AI Systems

While AI offers potential benefits for enhancing government cybersecurity capabilities [28], AI systems themselves introduce new and complex cybersecurity risks that must be managed.[95] The reliance on vast datasets, complex models, and interconnected infrastructure creates unique vulnerabilities that adversaries can exploit.[179] Securing AI in government is critical due to the sensitivity of the data handled and the potential impact of system compromise on public services and national security.[73]

Specific cybersecurity risks associated with AI systems include:

- **Data Poisoning:** Adversaries can intentionally corrupt the training data used to build AI models, introducing biases or backdoors that cause the model to malfunction or make incorrect predictions in specific situations.[72] This undermines the integrity of the AI system from its foundation.

- **Model Evasion and Manipulation:** Attackers can craft specific inputs designed to trick a deployed AI model into making incorrect classifications or predictions (evasion attacks).[173] Techniques like model inversion might allow attackers to extract sensitive information about the training data or the model itself.[173]

- **AI Infrastructure Compromise:** The underlying infrastructure supporting AI – including cloud platforms, data centers, edge devices, and networks – can be targeted by traditional cyberattacks, potentially disrupting AI services or compromising data.[179]

- **Malicious Use of AI:** Adversaries can leverage AI capabilities for nefarious purposes, such as creating more sophisticated phishing attacks, generating deepfakes for disinformation campaigns, automating malware development, or enhancing cyberattack capabilities.[125]

- **Data Breaches and Confidentiality Loss:** Compromises can lead to the theft or leakage of sensitive training data or operational data processed by AI systems, violating privacy and potentially exposing classified or proprietary information.[28] The opacity of some AI models can make detecting such breaches challenging.[95]

- **Supply Chain Vulnerabilities:** AI systems often rely on third-party software libraries, pre-trained models, or hardware components. Vulnerabilities within this supply chain can be exploited to compromise the entire AI system.[180]

Mitigating these risks requires a dedicated AI security strategy, integrating cybersecurity considerations throughout the AI lifecycle. Guidance from organizations like CISA (Cybersecurity and Infrastructure Security Agency) [106] and ENISA (European Union Agency for Cybersecurity) [180] emphasizes several key practices:

- **Robust Testing, Validation, and Verification (TEVV):** Rigorously testing AI models for performance, robustness against adversarial inputs, and security vulnerabilities before and after deployment.[13] This includes techniques like AI red teaming.[179]

- **Security by Design:** Integrating security considerations from the initial design phase of AI systems and infrastructure.[180]

- **Secure Data Management:** Implementing strong data governance, access controls, encryption, and monitoring for data used in AI systems.[56]

- **Continuous Monitoring:** Actively monitoring deployed AI systems for anomalous behavior, performance degradation, security threats, and potential data leakage.[56]

- **Incident Response Planning:** Developing specific plans to detect, respond to, and recover from AI-related security incidents.[68]

- **Supply Chain Security:** Assessing and managing the security risks associated with third-party components and vendors.[180]

- **Compliance Frameworks:** Adhering to relevant cybersecurity standards and frameworks, such as the NIST Cybersecurity Framework [68] or, in defense contexts, the Cybersecurity Maturity Model Certification (CMMC).[194]

Securing AI systems requires specialized expertise and a proactive, risk-based approach that recognizes the unique threat landscape associated with these powerful technologies.

Chapter 5

The Implementation Journey: Strategy, Challenges, and Change Management

Developing a National/Agency AI Native Strategy and Roadmap

Transitioning towards an AI Native government is not an organic process but requires deliberate, strategic planning and a clear roadmap.[128] Whether at a national or individual agency level, developing a comprehensive AI strategy is the crucial first step to guide investment, manage risks, and ensure that AI adoption aligns with public service goals and values.

The process of developing an AI strategy and roadmap involves several key elements:

1. **Define the Vision and "AI Ambition":** Leadership must articulate a clear vision for how AI will transform the organization or nation, defining the desired level of AI integration and impact.[102] This involves setting strategic goals aligned with overarching government priorities and mission needs [128], such as improving citizen services, enhancing efficiency, or strengthening security.

2. **Assess Readiness and Current State:** A thorough assessment of the organization's current AI maturity is necessary.[200] This includes evaluating existing data infrastructure, data quality and governance practices,

technological capabilities (cloud, compute), workforce skills, and organizational culture.[53] Identifying gaps between the current state and the desired future state is critical for planning.

3. **Identify and Prioritize Use Cases:** Brainstorming potential AI applications across various functions is important [93], but resources are finite. The strategy must prioritize use cases based on potential impact (e.g., citizen benefit, efficiency gains, mission enhancement), feasibility (technical, data availability), alignment with strategic goals, and risk levels.[93] Starting with high-value, lower-risk pilots can build momentum and provide valuable lessons.[93]

4. **Establish Governance and Ethical Guardrails:** The strategy must incorporate the development and implementation of a robust AI governance framework from the outset, defining ethical principles, risk management processes, accountability structures, and compliance requirements.[53]

5. **Develop a Phased Roadmap:** Create a practical, actionable roadmap outlining key milestones, timelines, required resources (budget, personnel, technology), and responsibilities for implementation.[128] This roadmap should be phased, often following an "ideation -> feasibility -> prioritization -> pilot -> scale" approach [93], allowing for learning and adaptation. Flexibility is key, given the rapid evolution of AI technology.[128]

6. **Secure Leadership Buy-in and Central Coordination:** Strong leadership commitment is essential for driving the strategy forward and overcoming organizational inertia.[200] Establishing a central coordinating body, such as an AI Center of Excellence (CoE) [129] or empowering a Chief AI

Officer (CAIO) [14], can ensure a unified approach, promote resource sharing, and enforce standards across the organization or government.[129]

Examples of government AI strategies, such as those mandated by US Executive Orders [1] or developed by specific agencies like the USDA [204] or states like Georgia [53], provide models. Frameworks from organizations like Gartner [128], Microsoft [202], and OGX [200] also offer structured approaches to roadmap development. A well-defined strategy and roadmap provide the necessary direction and discipline to navigate the complexities of AI Native transformation successfully.

Overcoming Implementation Hurdles: Legacy Systems, Budget Constraints, Data Silos

While the potential benefits of AI in government are significant, the path to implementation is fraught with practical challenges that can impede progress and derail initiatives.[148] Successfully navigating these hurdles is critical for realizing the AI Native vision. Key implementation challenges include:

- **Legacy Systems and Technical Debt:** Many government agencies operate on outdated IT infrastructure and legacy systems that were not designed for modern data processing or AI integration.[69] These systems often lack the necessary APIs, data formats, or processing power, creating significant technical barriers to deploying AI tools effectively. Overcoming this requires substantial modernization efforts, including migrating to cloud platforms, developing APIs for data access, and potentially replacing or refactoring core systems – tasks that are complex and costly.[28]

- **Budget Constraints and Procurement Issues:** AI initiatives require significant investment in technology, infrastructure, data preparation, and specialized talent.[148] Securing adequate funding can be difficult within constrained public sector budgets, especially when competing with other priorities.[26] Traditional government procurement processes can also be slow and ill-suited for acquiring rapidly evolving AI technologies, potentially leading to delays or reliance on outdated solutions.[132] Strategies to address this include demonstrating clear ROI from pilot projects [152], exploring innovative funding models, leveraging public-private partnerships [146], and reforming procurement practices to be more agile.[132]

- **Data Challenges (Quality, Silos, Governance):** As discussed previously, data issues are a major impediment. Poor data quality, lack of standardization, inconsistent formats, and data residing in isolated silos across different departments or agencies make it extremely difficult to aggregate, prepare, and utilize data effectively for AI.[41] Establishing robust data governance, investing in data quality improvement, and creating integrated data platforms are essential but resource-intensive prerequisites.[9] Privacy and security concerns further complicate data access and sharing.[59]

- **Skills Gaps and Workforce Readiness:** There is often a significant shortage of personnel within government agencies who possess the necessary AI, data science, and related technical skills to develop, deploy, and manage AI systems effectively.[49] Competition with the private sector for talent is fierce.[151] Furthermore, the existing workforce may lack basic AI literacy or resist changes to their workflows.[146] Addressing this requires substantial investment in training, upskilling, reskilling programs, and strategic recruitment efforts.[49]

- **Ethical Concerns and Public Trust:** Concerns about bias, fairness, transparency, privacy, and potential job displacement can create public and internal resistance to AI adoption.[25] Building and maintaining trust through ethical guidelines, transparent practices, and clear communication is crucial but challenging.[41]

- **Organizational Culture and Change Management:** Implementing AI often requires significant changes to existing processes, workflows, and organizational structures. Resistance to change, bureaucratic inertia, and lack of leadership buy-in can hinder adoption.[25] Effective change management strategies are essential.[25]

Overcoming these hurdles requires a holistic approach involving strategic planning, sustained investment, strong leadership, workforce development, robust governance, and effective change management. Starting small with pilot projects, demonstrating value early, and fostering collaboration can help build momentum and navigate these complex challenges.[93]

Workforce Transformation: Skilling, Reskilling, and Attracting Talent

The successful implementation and operation of an AI Native Government depend critically on having a workforce equipped with the necessary skills and understanding to leverage AI technologies effectively and responsibly.[49] However, significant skills gaps currently exist within most public sector organizations, posing a major barrier to AI adoption.[49] Addressing this requires a multi-faceted workforce transformation strategy encompassing skilling, reskilling, and talent attraction.

Key components include:

- **AI Literacy for All:** Foundational AI literacy needs to be established across the entire workforce, not just technical staff. Employees at all levels need to understand the basic concepts of AI, its potential applications within their domain, its limitations, and the ethical considerations involved.[53] This fosters a better understanding of AI's role and facilitates collaboration between technical and non-technical staff.

- **Upskilling and Reskilling Programs:** Targeted training programs are needed to equip existing employees with new skills relevant to the AI era.[53] This includes:

  - *Technical Skills:* Training for data scientists, AI engineers, developers, and IT staff on specific AI tools, platforms (e.g., cloud AI services), programming languages, data management techniques, and MLOps practices.[210]

  - *Domain-Specific AI Skills:* Training for public servants in specific domains (e.g., healthcare, law enforcement, policy analysis) on how to effectively use AI tools relevant to their work, interpret AI outputs critically, and ensure responsible application.[208]

  - *Ethical and Governance Skills:* Training on AI ethics, bias detection, privacy regulations, risk management frameworks, and responsible AI principles for all involved in AI projects.[68]

  - *Leadership Skills:* Training for managers and executives on how to lead AI initiatives, manage change, foster an AI-ready culture, and make strategic decisions about AI adoption.[208] Initiatives like the GSA's AI Training Series 211, Microsoft's Civil Servants Academy [209], Portugal's AI Business School AP [209], and programs like the Partnership for Public Service's AI Government Leadership Program [208] provide models for government AI training. Leveraging partnerships with academic institutions and private sector providers can scale these efforts.[199]

- **Attracting and Retaining AI Talent:** Governments face challenges competing with the private sector for scarce AI and data science talent due to factors like compensation and hiring processes.[49] Strategies to attract talent include:

  - *Streamlining Hiring:* Modernizing recruitment processes to evaluate technical skills effectively and reduce hiring timelines.[213]

  - *Competitive Compensation and Benefits:* Reviewing pay scales and benefits packages to be more competitive for in-demand roles.[49]

  - *Mission-Driven Appeal:* Emphasizing the opportunity to work on impactful public service missions.[208]

  - *Flexible Work Arrangements:* Offering modern work environments and potentially flexible arrangements (though recent trends may limit this [27]).

  - *Creating Dedicated AI Roles/Units:* Establishing clear career paths and dedicated units like AI Centers of Excellence or the AI Corps [129] can attract specialists. Initiatives like the USDS "tour of duty" model can bring in external expertise for limited periods.[27]

- **Developing AI-Related Occupational Categories:** Formalizing job roles and occupational series related to AI within government HR systems helps in recruitment, development, and workforce planning.[169]

Building an AI-ready workforce is not a one-time effort but requires continuous investment in learning and development to keep pace with the rapid evolution of AI technology.[207] It is essential for ensuring that AI is used effectively, ethically, and sustainably to enhance government operations and public services.

Change Management: Fostering an AI-Ready Culture

Technological implementation is only one part of the AI Native transformation; equally important, and often more challenging, is managing the human and organizational changes required.[25] Successfully integrating AI into government workflows necessitates effective change management strategies to overcome resistance, build buy-in, and foster a culture that embraces data-driven innovation while upholding public service values.

Key aspects of change management for AI adoption include:

- **Leadership Commitment and Vision:** Strong, visible commitment from senior leadership is crucial.[200] Leaders must articulate a clear vision for how AI will benefit the agency and its constituents, communicate this vision consistently, and champion the necessary changes.[199] Experimenting with AI tools themselves can demonstrate commitment.[202]

- **Addressing Workforce Concerns:** Employees may fear job displacement, deskilling, or loss of autonomy due to AI and automation.[25] Change management must proactively address these concerns through transparent communication, emphasizing AI's role in augmenting human capabilities rather than wholesale replacement.[25] Highlighting how AI can reduce tedious tasks and free up time for more meaningful work can help build acceptance.[25] Public service employees are often optimistic about AI's potential if approached correctly.[214]

- **Stakeholder Engagement and Communication:** Engaging employees, managers, union representatives, and other internal stakeholders early and often in the planning and implementation process is vital.146 Seeking input, incorporating feedback, and maintaining open communication channels helps build ownership and reduce resistance.[112]

- **Training and Support:** Providing adequate training not only builds necessary skills (as discussed above) but also increases employee confidence and comfort with new AI-powered tools and processes.[202] Ongoing support mechanisms are needed as employees adapt.[148]

- **Redesigning Workflows and Roles:** AI implementation often requires rethinking and redesigning existing workflows and job roles.[214] This involves identifying tasks suitable for automation or augmentation and redefining human roles to focus on areas requiring judgment, creativity, empathy, and strategic thinking.[25] This requires careful planning and collaboration with affected staff.[214]

- **Fostering a Data-Driven and Experimental Culture:** Encouraging a mindset that values data-informed decision-making, experimentation, and continuous learning is essential for AI success.[9] This involves creating safe spaces for piloting new AI tools (e.g., AI sandboxes [53]), learning from failures, and iterating based on results.[93]

- **Integrating Governance and Ethics:** Embedding ethical considerations and governance processes into the change management strategy ensures that AI adoption aligns with public service values and maintains trust.[146]

Change management is not a separate activity but an integral part of the AI implementation journey. Neglecting the human and cultural dimensions significantly increases the risk of AI projects failing to achieve their objectives or encountering strong internal resistance.[25] A thoughtful, empathetic, and strategic approach to change is required to build an AI-ready organization.

Public-Private Partnerships and International Collaboration

Achieving the ambitious goals of AI Native Government often requires collaboration beyond the boundaries of individual agencies or even national governments. Public-private partnerships (PPPs) and international cooperation play vital roles in accelerating innovation, accessing expertise, sharing best practices, and addressing the global nature of AI challenges.

- **Public-Private Partnerships (PPPs):** Governments often lack the specialized technical expertise, cutting-edge research capabilities, or agile development processes found in the private sector and academia.[3] PPPs can bridge this gap by:

  o *Accessing Technology and Expertise:* Partnering with tech companies (large providers like Microsoft [80], Google [82], AWS [76], Oracle [80], or specialized AI firms [121]) provides access to advanced AI platforms, tools, and technical talent.[28] Consulting firms (e.g., Accenture [47], Deloitte 104, BCG [218], McKinsey [215]) also play a significant role in strategy and implementation.[218]

  o Driving Innovation: Collaborations can spur research and development tailored to public sector needs, foster GovTech ecosystems, and support pilot projects.[11]

  o Workforce Development: Partnerships can support training and upskilling programs for public servants.[199] However, PPPs require careful management to ensure alignment with public interest, maintain accountability, avoid vendor lock-in [131], and protect sensitive government data.[223] Clear contractual terms and robust governance are essential.[132]

- International Collaboration: AI development and deployment have global implications, necessitating international cooperation.[18] Key areas for collaboration include:

  o *Developing Shared Standards and Principles:* Working through international fora like the OECD 18, GPAI [199], UN bodies [225], G7/G20 [19], and bilateral initiatives [224] to establish common norms, definitions, and ethical guidelines for trustworthy AI.[13] This promotes interoperability and facilitates responsible AI governance globally.[162]

  o *Sharing Best Practices and Lessons Learned:* Exchanging knowledge and experiences regarding AI strategies, implementation challenges, governance approaches, and use cases helps accelerate progress and avoid duplication of effort.[19] Initiatives like the AI Safety Institutes Network facilitate this.[143]

  o *Addressing Transnational Risks:* Collaborating on managing shared risks such as cross-border cybersecurity threats, the spread of AI-driven disinformation, or ensuring AI safety for globally deployed systems.[179]

  o *Joint Research and Development:* Pooling resources for large-scale AI research projects, particularly those addressing global challenges like climate change or health.[199]

Effective collaboration requires sustained diplomatic engagement, participation in international standard-setting bodies, and a willingness to share information while safeguarding national interests.[13] Both PPPs and international cooperation are crucial enablers for governments seeking to navigate the complexities and harness the full potential of the AI revolution.

Chapter 6

The Future of AI Native Government

Long-Term Societal Implications and Governance Challenges

The transition to AI Native Government is not merely a technological upgrade but a profound societal shift with potentially far-reaching and long-term consequences.46 While AI offers immense potential for public good, its deep integration into governance raises critical questions about the future shape of society, the economy, and democracy itself, demanding ongoing foresight and adaptive governance.[125]

Key long-term implications and associated governance challenges include:

- **Economic Transformation and Inequality:** AI-driven automation is expected to significantly impact labor markets, potentially displacing jobs in both manual and cognitive fields.[34] While new jobs may be created, there's a risk of increased unemployment, wage stagnation for certain skills, and widening economic inequality.[48] This necessitates proactive government policies for workforce transition, reskilling/upskilling, social safety nets, and potentially rethinking taxation models (e.g., taxing capital vs. labor).[13] The concentration of AI development and economic benefits in a few companies or countries could also exacerbate global inequalities.[125]

- Impact on Social Fabric and Human Interaction: Increased reliance on AI for communication, service delivery, and even companionship (e.g., therapeutic robots [239]) could alter social dynamics, potentially reducing human-to-human interaction and impacting cognitive skills or critical thinking.[235] The pervasive nature of AI could reshape cultural norms and values.[241]

- **Erosion of Privacy and Expansion of Surveillance:** AI's ability to analyze vast datasets, including biometric data (facial recognition, gait analysis) and online activities, significantly enhances surveillance capabilities for both state and non-state actors.[45] This poses profound risks to individual privacy, freedom of expression, and association, potentially enabling more effective state control or oppression, especially in authoritarian contexts.20 Strong legal safeguards and ethical boundaries are crucial.[124]

- **Misinformation, Disinformation, and Trust:** AI, particularly generative AI, can create highly realistic deepfakes and automate the spread of false or misleading information at scale, posing significant threats to public discourse, trust in institutions (including media and government), and democratic processes.[18] Countering this requires technological solutions (e.g., content authentication), media literacy initiatives, and platform accountability.

- **Complexity and Control (Existential Risk Debates):** As AI systems become more complex and autonomous, concerns arise about maintaining meaningful human control, the potential for unexpected emergent behaviors, and, in the long term, the speculative risks associated with artificial general intelligence (AGI) or superintelligence that could potentially pose existential threats.[28] While highly debated, these long-term safety considerations inform current research and governance discussions.[125]

- **Environmental Impact:** The significant energy and water consumption required for training and running large AI models, particularly in data centers, raises environmental sustainability concerns that need to be addressed through energy-efficient hardware, renewable energy sources, and responsible infrastructure development.[90]

Governing these long-term impacts requires adaptive, forward-looking approaches.[234] This involves investing in strategic foresight capabilities within government [234], promoting multi-stakeholder dialogue on societal values and AI trajectories [12], fostering international cooperation on global norms and risk mitigation 19, and developing flexible regulatory frameworks that can evolve alongside the technology.[46] The challenge is to proactively shape AI's trajectory towards beneficial outcomes while anticipating and mitigating potential harms before they become entrenched.[233]

Speculative Applications: Digital Twins and Beyond

Looking further into the future, AI Native Government could leverage increasingly sophisticated technologies, moving beyond current applications towards more speculative but potentially transformative capabilities. One prominent example is the concept of Digital Twins.

A Digital Twin is a dynamic virtual representation of a physical entity, process, or system that is continuously updated with real-time data from its physical counterpart.[130] Unlike static simulations, digital twins allow for ongoing monitoring, analysis, prediction, and optimization of the real-world system.[248] AI plays a crucial role in building, analyzing, and interacting with these complex virtual replicas.[130]

Potential applications in the public sector include:

- **Smart Cities and Urban Planning:** Creating digital twins of entire cities or regions to simulate traffic flow, energy consumption, environmental impacts (e.g., air quality, flood risk), infrastructure performance, and the effects of new developments or policies.[248] The country of Singapore and Boston city are examples exploring this.[250] This allows for optimized urban planning, resource management, and disaster preparedness.[249]

- **Infrastructure Management:** Developing digital twins of critical infrastructure assets like bridges, power grids, or water systems to monitor their condition in real-time, predict maintenance needs, simulate stress responses, and optimize operations.[130] NASA uses digital twins for facility management.[130]

- **Healthcare and Public Health:** Creating digital twins of healthcare systems to optimize hospital operations (e.g., patient flow, bed allocation) [248], or even personalized digital twins of individuals to simulate treatment responses, predict disease risks, and tailor preventative care.[248]

- **Defense and National Security:** Using digital twins to model complex military equipment (e.g., aircraft [249]) for predictive maintenance and readiness assessment, simulate battlefield scenarios for training and strategy development [157], or model satellite operations and orbital environments.[249]

- **Policy Simulation:** Creating digital twins of economies or specific social systems to test the potential impacts of different policy interventions with greater realism and granularity than traditional models.[250]

- **"Crystal Agencies":** Conceptualizing a digital twin of an entire government agency to provide complete transparency into its operations, processes, information flows, and resource allocation, enabling optimization and accountability.[250]

The development and deployment of digital twins rely heavily on advancements in sensor technology (IoT), data integration, high-performance computing, and AI/ML algorithms.[130] Key challenges include ensuring data quality and real-time synchronization, managing the complexity of the models, guaranteeing cybersecurity (as attacks on a digital twin could affect the physical counterpart [248]), ensuring interoperability between different twins [130], and addressing ethical concerns related to accuracy, bias, and privacy, especially for personalized twins.[248]

Beyond digital twins, other speculative applications might involve more advanced forms of AI-driven automation, highly personalized proactive public services, AI-mediated citizen deliberation platforms, or even AI systems playing more direct roles in governance functions, though these raise profound questions about human agency and democratic control.[252] While speculative, exploring these future possibilities helps inform current strategic thinking about the long-term trajectory of AI in government.

The Evolving Citizen-Government Relationship

The integration of AI into government operations has the potential to fundamentally reshape the relationship between the government and its citizens.[21] This evolution presents both opportunities for enhanced engagement and service delivery, and risks related to trust, equity, and citizen agency.

Potential positive transformations include:

- **Increased Responsiveness and Personalization:** AI can enable governments to move away from one-size-fits-all service delivery towards more personalized interactions tailored to individual needs and circumstances.[21] AI-powered assistants can provide instant responses and guidance 24/7 29, while predictive analytics might allow for proactive service offerings.[21] This could lead to a more citizen-centric government experience, meeting expectations set by the private sector.[21]

- **Improved Accessibility and Convenience:** AI can simplify complex government processes, make information easier to find and understand (e.g., through NLP summaries or chatbots [107]), provide multilingual support [29], and offer services through multiple digital channels accessible anytime, anywhere.[30] This can reduce administrative burdens for citizens.[8]

- **Enhanced Transparency and Engagement:** AI tools can analyze citizen feedback and sentiment from various sources, providing governments with better insights into public opinion and needs.[28] Theoretically, AI could support more direct forms of citizen participation or deliberation, although this remains largely speculative. Transparency initiatives, like public AI inventories, can increase visibility into government operations.[43]

However, significant risks and challenges accompany this evolution:

- **Erosion of Trust:** If AI systems are perceived as biased, unfair, inaccurate, opaque, or insecure, or if their deployment leads to negative consequences (e.g., wrongful denial of benefits), public trust in government can be severely damaged.[41] High-profile failures can have lasting impacts.[41]

- **Digital Divide and Equity Concerns:** Reliance on AI-driven digital services may disadvantage citizens with limited digital access or literacy, potentially exacerbating existing inequalities.48 Ensuring equitable access and designing inclusive systems is critical.

- **Privacy Concerns:** Personalized services require the collection and analysis of significant amounts of citizen data, raising privacy concerns and requiring robust data protection measures.[62] Surveillance applications of AI further intensify these worries.[116]

- **Reduced Human Interaction and Empathy:** Over-reliance on automated systems might lead to a less humane and empathetic government, particularly in sensitive areas like social services or healthcare where personal interaction is valued.[75] Finding the right balance between automation and human touchpoints is essential.[33]

- **Manipulation and Disinformation:** AI's potential to generate targeted messaging or deepfakes could be used to manipulate public opinion or interfere with citizen understanding of government actions.[45]

Navigating this evolving relationship requires governments to prioritize citizen-centric design [33], actively build and maintain trust through transparency and accountability [43], ensure ethical and equitable deployment [146], protect privacy rigorously [64], and consciously design for human-AI collaboration that enhances, rather than diminishes, the human element of public service.[8] The future relationship will depend heavily on the choices made today regarding AI governance and implementation.

The Future of Democracy in the Age of AI

The proliferation of AI technologies presents profound questions and potential challenges for the future functioning of democratic institutions and processes.[126] While AI offers potential avenues to enhance certain aspects of governance, it also introduces significant risks that could undermine democratic values, participation, and stability.

Potential opportunities for strengthening democracy include:

- **Enhanced Government Efficiency and Responsiveness:** AI could improve the delivery of public services and make government operations more efficient, potentially increasing citizen satisfaction and trust in institutions.[43]

- **Improved Policy Analysis:** AI's ability to analyze complex data and simulate policy outcomes could lead to more evidence-based and effective policymaking, better aligning government actions with public needs.[34]

- **Increased Citizen Engagement (Potential):** AI tools could theoretically facilitate greater citizen participation by simplifying access to information, analyzing public input more effectively, or enabling new forms of digital deliberation [39], although realizing this potential requires careful design.

However, the risks to democracy posed by AI are substantial and widely acknowledged:

- **Misinformation and Disinformation:** Generative AI enables the creation and rapid dissemination of highly realistic deepfakes (audio, video, images) and sophisticated disinformation campaigns at scale.[125] This can manipulate public opinion, sow discord, interfere in elections, and erode trust in credible information sources and institutions.[45]

- **Manipulation and Polarization:** AI algorithms used by social media platforms and political campaigns can micro-target voters with personalized messaging, potentially exploiting psychological vulnerabilities and amplifying political polarization.[242] Automated bot networks can further distort online discourse.[243]

- **Erosion of Truth and Trust:** The proliferation of synthetic media makes it harder for citizens to distinguish truth from falsehood, potentially leading to widespread skepticism even towards genuine information and undermining the shared factual basis necessary for democratic debate.[126] Politicians may exploit this by falsely claiming real evidence is a deepfake.[255]

- **Surveillance and Chilling Effects:** Government use of AI for surveillance (e.g., facial recognition, social media monitoring) can chill free expression, association, and dissent, core tenets of democracy.[116]

- **Algorithmic Bias and Discrimination:** Biased AI systems used in government decision-making (e.g., criminal justice, resource allocation) can perpetuate systemic inequalities and undermine principles of fairness and equal treatment under the law.[44]

- **Reduced Human Involvement in Governance:** Over-reliance on opaque algorithmic decision-making could diminish the role of human judgment and public deliberation in governance, potentially leading to "algocracy" where systems, not citizens, dictate outcomes.[242]

- **Concentration of Power:** The development and control of powerful AI systems are concentrated in a few large tech companies, raising concerns about corporate influence over the digital public sphere and democratic processes.[126]

Safeguarding democracy in the age of AI requires a multi-pronged approach. This includes developing regulations for transparency in AI-generated content (especially political advertising) [243], holding platforms accountable for mitigating the spread of harmful disinformation [243], investing in media literacy, promoting research into AI's societal impacts, ensuring robust governance and oversight of AI use by governments [256], and fostering international cooperation on norms for responsible AI deployment.[126] The challenge is to harness AI's potential benefits while actively defending democratic principles against its inherent risks.

International Perspectives and the Global AI Landscape (UK, Singapore, Estonia)

The development and governance of AI Native Government is not occurring in isolation; nations worldwide are formulating strategies, launching initiatives, and grappling with similar challenges, creating a dynamic global landscape. Examining the approaches of other leading digital governments provides valuable insights and benchmarks.

- **United Kingdom (UK):** The UK government has expressed strong ambitions to be a global AI leader, focusing on boosting economic growth and improving public services through AI adoption.142 Key initiatives include the AI Opportunities Action Plan [217], establishing a National Data Library [257], and creating an AI Safety Institute (initially focused on safety, now more on security [217]). The government is actively pursuing public sector AI implementation, with numerous initiatives across departments [142] and partnerships with AI providers like Anthropic to develop citizen-facing services (e.g., chatbots).[217] However, the UK has opted for a relatively light-touch regulatory approach, relying on existing regulators and principles-based guidance (e.g., the AI Playbook [217]) rather than comprehensive legislation like the EU AI Act. This approach aims to foster innovation but raises concerns about ensuring trustworthiness and mitigating risks without stronger enforcement.[217] There are ongoing debates about balancing innovation with data protection and copyright laws.[257]

- **Singapore**: Consistently ranked as a leader in digital government and AI readiness, Singapore adopts a pragmatic and proactive approach focused on building trust and harnessing AI for public good.[142] Key elements include a national AI strategy, significant investment in AI research and talent (e.g., through GovTech [29]), and a strong emphasis on AI governance and ethics. Singapore has launched initiatives like AI Verify (a testing framework and toolkit) and the AI Verify Foundation to promote responsible AI development and testing.[143] They actively engage in international collaboration, piloting AI assurance practices with partners like Japan [143] and participating in global dialogues. Use cases include AI-powered chatbots for citizen services ("Ask Jamie" 29), exploring GenAI for scam detection and law enforcement [143], and leveraging AI for

77

personalized services and efficient operations.43 Singapore's approach emphasizes practical implementation, industry partnership, and building international consensus on AI safety and governance.[143]

- **Estonia:** A pioneer in e-governance and digital government, Estonia views AI as a natural evolution of its digital society.[31] Their strategy focuses on integrating AI seamlessly into public services to enhance efficiency and citizen experience.[31] They have implemented numerous AI applications ("krattAI") across sectors like healthcare (predictive analytics), transportation (traffic management), and administration (chatbots).[31] A notable recent initiative is "AI Leap," a public-private partnership aiming to integrate AI tools and skills into the entire education system by 2025-2026, providing free access to leading AI applications for students and teachers.[144] Estonia emphasizes a human-centric approach, ensuring AI systems operate under human oversight and adhere to ethical principles. Their success builds on a strong digital foundation (e.g., secure digital identity, data exchange layer X-Road) and a culture of digital innovation.[31] Challenges include ensuring data privacy and managing public perception.[31]

These examples illustrate different national strategies – the UK's focus on innovation and market-led solutions within a lighter regulatory framework, Singapore's emphasis on governance, trust-building, and international standards, and Estonia's integration of AI as a core component of its established digital government. Learning from these diverse approaches – their successes, challenges, and specific policy choices – is crucial for any government charting its own path towards an AI Native future. International collaboration and sharing of best practices remain vital in navigating this complex global transformation.[19]

Chapter 7

Conclusion: Charting the Course for Responsible AI Native Transformation

Synthesizing Key Themes and Challenges

The journey towards an AI Native Government represents a fundamental transformation, moving beyond incremental digitization to a state where artificial intelligence is intrinsically woven into the fabric of public administration, service delivery, and policy-making. This book has outlined a potential blueprint for understanding this transition, exploring its definition, foundational requirements, diverse applications, critical governance needs, implementation hurdles, and future implications.

Several key themes emerge from this exploration:

1. **The AI Native Paradigm Shift:** This is not merely about adopting new tools but requires a systemic change in architecture, processes, culture, and skills, demanding a holistic, whole-of-government approach.

2. **The Data Imperative:** High-quality, well-governed, secure, and accessible data is the absolute prerequisite for effective and responsible AI deployment in government. Neglecting the data foundation is a primary cause of failure.

3. **Transformative Potential:** AI offers significant opportunities to enhance government efficiency, personalize citizen services, enable data-driven policy,

optimize resource allocation, and address complex societal challenges more effectively, and to in fact reimagine the model and functioning of a government.

4. **Governance as an Enabler:** Robust governance frameworks, grounded in ethical principles like transparency, fairness, accountability, and privacy, are not obstacles to innovation but essential enablers for building public trust and ensuring AI serves the public good.

5. **Implementation Complexity:** The path to AI Native is fraught with challenges, including legacy systems, budget constraints, data silos, workforce skills gaps, cybersecurity risks, and the need for effective change management.

6. **Societal and Democratic Implications:** The widespread adoption of AI in government carries profound long-term implications for the economy, employment, social interaction, privacy, and the very functioning of governments and democracy, requiring careful foresight and proactive management.

The core challenge lies in navigating the inherent tensions within this transformation: balancing innovation with risk, efficiency with equity, personalization with privacy, automation with human judgment, and national interests with global cooperation.

Recommendations for Policymakers and Public Sector Leaders

Based on the analysis presented, several strategic recommendations emerge for policymakers and public sector leaders aiming to navigate the transition to an AI Native Government responsibly and effectively:

1. **Develop a Clear, Values-Driven AI Strategy:** Articulate a national or government agency-specific vision for AI Native transformation, explicitly grounding it in public service values and ethical principles. Prioritize use cases based on public value and feasibility, and create an adaptive roadmap with clear milestones.

2. **Prioritize Data Modernization and Governance:** Treat data as a strategic asset. Invest significantly in breaking down data silos, improving data quality, establishing robust data governance frameworks (including appointing CDOs), and ensuring data security and privacy compliance. Make "AI-ready" data a top priority.

3. **Build Integrated and Resilient Infrastructure:** Invest strategically in a hybrid infrastructure combining cloud scalability, necessary compute power (HPC/GPUs), and edge capabilities, underpinned by robust networking. Ensure compliance with relevant security standards (e.g., FedRAMP, CMMC where applicable).

4. **Establish Comprehensive and Adaptive AI Governance:** Implement a formal governance framework tailored to the public sector context, drawing from international best practices (e.g., OECD, NIST, EU AI Act principles). Embed mechanisms for risk management, ethical review, bias mitigation, transparency, accountability, and human oversight throughout the AI lifecycle. Ensure governance evolves with technology.

5. **Invest Heavily in Workforce Transformation:** Launch comprehensive AI literacy programs for all staff. Develop targeted upskilling and reskilling initiatives for technical, domain-specific, ethical, and leadership competencies

related to AI. Implement strategies to attract and retain specialized AI talent.

6. **Champion Change Management and Foster an AI-Ready Culture:** Lead the cultural shift required for AI adoption. Communicate transparently, address workforce concerns proactively, engage stakeholders, redesign workflows collaboratively, and encourage responsible experimentation and learning.

7. **Mandate Transparency and Public Engagement:** Implement measures like public AI use case inventories and clear explanations of AI systems. Actively engage citizens and civil society in shaping AI priorities and governance to build and maintain public trust. Provide clear mechanisms for redress.

8. **Focus on Human-AI Collaboration:** Design AI systems to augment, not necessarily replace, human capabilities. Preserve human judgment and oversight, especially in high-stakes decisions, ensuring AI serves as a tool to empower public servants and enhance citizen interactions.

9. **Promote Interoperability and Collaboration:** Foster data sharing and system interoperability across government agencies through open standards and APIs. Engage actively in public-private partnerships and international collaborations to share knowledge, develop common standards, and address shared challenges.

10. **Invest in Strategic Foresight:** Develop institutional capacity to anticipate the long-term societal, economic, and democratic implications of AI, enabling proactive policy responses and adaptive governance.

Final Thoughts on the AI Native Future

The concept of an AI Native Government offers a compelling vision for a more efficient, effective, responsive, and intelligent public sector. It holds the promise of transforming service delivery, tackling complex challenges with greater insight, and potentially rebuilding trust between citizens and the state.

However, this transformation is neither simple nor guaranteed. It requires navigating significant technical, organizational, ethical, and societal hurdles. The risks associated with bias, privacy, security, accountability, and unintended consequences are substantial and demand constant vigilance. The journey necessitates not just technological investment but also a fundamental rethinking of government processes, workforce skills, and governance structures.

Ultimately, the success of the AI Native Government will hinge on the ability of leaders to steer this powerful technology responsibly. It requires a commitment to placing human values – fairness, transparency, accountability, privacy, and dignity – at the center of AI design and deployment. It demands a focus on building public trust through openness and engagement. And it necessitates a forward-looking perspective that anticipates and shapes the long-term impacts of AI on society and democracy. Charting this course requires wisdom, collaboration, and a steadfast commitment to ensuring that the AI Native future serves the interests of all citizens.

End Notes

1. Artificial Intelligence for the American People - Trump White House Archives, accessed May 3, 2025, https://trumpwhitehouse.archives.gov/ai/

2. Digital Government Strategy - United States Department of State, accessed May 3, 2025,

   https://www.state.gov/digital-government-strategy

3. Rethinking AI for Good Governance | American Academy of Arts and Sciences, accessed May 3, 2025, https://www.amacad.org/publication/daedalus/rethinking-ai-good-governance

4. Artificial intelligence in government: Concepts, standards, and a unified framework - arXiv, accessed May 3, 2025, https://arxiv.org/pdf/2210.17218

5. A detailed study of the AI Native concept - Ericsson, accessed May 3, 2025, https://www.ericsson.com/en/reports-and-papers/white-papers/ai-native

6. The Algorithmic State Architecture (ASA): An Integrated Framework for AI-Enabled Government - arXiv, accessed May 3, 2025, http://www.arxiv.org/pdf/2503.08725

7. GovTech: The New Frontier in Digital Government Transformation - World Bank, accessed May 3, 2025, https://pubdocs.worldbank.org/en/805211612215188198/GovTech-Guidance-Note-1-The-Frontier.pdf

8. A Cheat Sheet for AI in Government - Code for America, accessed May 3, 2025, https://codeforamerica.org/news/a-cheat-sheet-for-ai-in-government/

9. Google AI: Data Access, Strategy & Implementation for Gov, accessed May 3, 2025, https://cloud.google.com/blog/topics/public-sector/the-three-pillars-of-data-driven-government

10. Public Sector Solutions | Databricks Platform, accessed May 3, 2025, https://www.databricks.com/solutions/industries/public-sector

11. New Paper: The Algorithmic State Architecture (ASA) – An Integrated Framework for AI-Enabled Government - Data for Policy, accessed May 3, 2025, https://dataforpolicy.org/new-paper-the-algorithmic-state-architecture-asa-a-blueprint-for-ai-enabled-government/

12. What is AI Governance? - IBM, accessed May 3, 2025, https://www.ibm.com/think/topics/ai-governance

13. Highlights of the 2023 Executive Order on Artificial Intelligence for Congress, accessed May 3, 2025, https://crsreports.congress.gov/product/pdf/R/R47843

14. AI Executive Order Explained: Principles, Provisions ... - Aqua Security, accessed May 3, 2025, https://www.aquasec.com/cloud-native-academy/application-security/ai-executive-order/

15. Ethical concerns mount as AI takes bigger decision-making role - Harvard Gazette, accessed May 3, 2025,

https://news.harvard.edu/gazette/story/2020/10/ethical-concerns-mount-as-ai-takes-bigger-decision-making-role/

16. Understanding AI Safety: Principles, Frameworks, and Best Practices - Tigera.io, accessed May 3, 2025, https://www.tigera.io/learn/guides/llm-security/ai-safety/

17. Principles of Artificial Intelligence Ethics for the Intelligence Community - INTEL.gov, accessed May 3, 2025, https://www.intelligence.gov/principles-of-artificial-intelligence-ethics-for-the-intelligence-community

18. AI principles - OECD, accessed May 3, 2025, https://www.oecd.org/en/topics/ai-principles.html

19. AI Principles Overview - OECD.AI, accessed May 3, 2025, https://oecd.ai/en/ai-principles

20. Memorandum on Advancing the United States' Leadership in Artificial Intelligence; Harnessing Artificial Intelligence to Fulfill National Security Objectives; and Fostering the Safety, Security, and Trustworthiness of Artificial Intelligence, accessed May 3, 2025, https://bidenwhitehouse.archives.gov/briefing-room/presidential-actions/2024/10/24/memorandum-on-advancing-the-united-states-leadership-in-artificial-intelligence-harnessing-artificial-intelligence-to-fulfill-national-security-objectives-and-fostering-the-safety-security/

21. Governing in the Age of AI: A New Model to Transform the State - Tony Blair Institute, accessed May 3, 2025, https://institute.global/insights/politics-and-governance/governing-in-the-age-of-ai-a-new-model-to-transform-the-state

22. Use cases of Robotic Process Automation in Government - A3Logics, accessed May 3, 2025, https://www.a3logics.com/blog/use-cases-of-rpa-in-government/

23. Will automation and AI help bring economy and efficiency to the public sector, accessed May 3, 2025, https://trinus.com/will-automation-and-ai-help-bring-economy-and-efficiency-to-the-public-sector/

24. Driving Government Efficiency with AI-Powered Process Automation - TechSur Solutions, accessed May 3, 2025, https://techsur.solutions/driving-government-efficiency-with-ai-powered-process-automation/

25. Unlocking the Power of AI - Public Sector Network, accessed May 3, 2025, https://publicsectornetwork.com/insight/unlocking-the-power-of-ai-how-government-can-leverage-data-for-better-citizen-services

26. The Budgeting Process: Governments Find Power in AI - National League of Cities, accessed May 3, 2025, https://www.nlc.org/article/2025/02/18/the-budgeting-process-governments-find-power-in-ai/

27. From Meme to Machine: How the US DOGE Service Can Help Reimagine US Government for the Age of AI - Tony Blair Institute, accessed May 3, 2025, https://institute.global/insights/tech-and-digitalisation/how-the-us-doge-service-can-help-reimagine-us-government-for-the-age-of-ai

28. AI in government: Top use cases - IBM, accessed May 3, 2025, https://www.ibm.com/think/topics/ai-in-government

29. How Governments are Using AI: 8 Real-World Case Studies, accessed May 3, 2025, https://blog.govnet.co.uk/technology/ai-in-government-case-studies

30. AI use cases in government that improve the citizen experience - The Future of Commerce, accessed May 3, 2025, https://www.the-future-of-commerce.com/2025/02/20/examples-of-ai-use-cases-in-government/

31. Case Study: AI Implementation in the Government of Estonia - Public Sector Network, accessed May 3, 2025, https://publicsectornetwork.com/insight/case-study-ai-implementation-in-the-government-of-estonia

32. 5 AI Trends Shaping the Future of Public Sector in 2025 | Google Cloud Blog, accessed May 3, 2025, https://cloud.google.com/blog/topics/public-sector/5-ai-trends-shaping-the-future-of-the-public-sector-in-2025

33. Artificial Intelligence for Citizen Services and Government - Harvard Ash Center, accessed May 3, 2025, https://ash.harvard.edu/wp-content/uploads/2024/02/artificial_intelligence_for_citizen_services.pdf

34. Will AI replace policymakers? - Joseph Rowntree Foundation, accessed May 3, 2025, https://www.jrf.org.uk/ai-for-public-good/will-ai-replace-policymakers

35. Artificial Intelligence in Economic Policymaking, accessed May 3, 2025, https://www.apec.org/docs/default-source/publications/2022/11/artificial-intelligence-in-

economic-policymaking/222_psu_artificial-intelligence-in-economic-policymaking.pdf

36. What is Predictive Analytics Governance - Explanation & Examples | Secoda, accessed May 3, 2025, https://www.secoda.co/glossary/what-is-predictive-analytics-governance

37. Harnessing the Power of Predictive Analytics for Data-Driven Decision-Making in the Public Sector - MicroStrategy, accessed May 3, 2025, https://www.strategysoftware.com/blog/harnessing-the-power-of-predictive-analytics-for-data-driven-decision-making-in-the-public-sector

38. Guide to Data-Driven Policy in the Public Sector - Number Analytics, accessed May 3, 2025, https://www.numberanalytics.com/blog/data-driven-policy-public-sector-guide

39. The Role of AI in Public Policy Making [2025] - DigitalDefynd, accessed May 3, 2025, https://digitaldefynd.com/IQ/role-of-ai-in-public-policy-making/

40. Leveraging AI to Transform Macroeconomic and Fiscal Policymaking in Latin America and the Caribbean - Blog del Banco Interamericano de Desarrollo, accessed May 3, 2025, https://blogs.iadb.org/gestion-fiscal/en/ai-to-transform-macroeconomic-and-fiscal-policymaking/

41. For AI to make government work better, reduce risk and increase transparency - Brookings Institution, accessed May 3, 2025, https://www.brookings.edu/articles/for-ai-to-make-government-work-better-reduce-risk-and-increase-transparency/

42. New Federal Agency Policies and Protocols for Artificial Intelligence Utilization and Procurement Can Provide Useful Guidance for Private Entities - Workforce Bulletin, accessed May 3, 2025, https://www.workforcebulletin.com/new-federal-agency-policies-and-protocols-for-artificial-intelligence-utilization-and-procurement-can-provide-useful-guidance-for-private-entities

43. To Help Rebuild Public Trust in Government, Harness AI, accessed May 3, 2025, https://www.cigionline.org/articles/to-help-rebuild-public-trust-in-government-harness-ai/

44. annenberg.usc.edu, accessed May 3, 2025, https://annenberg.usc.edu/research/center-public-relations/usc-annenberg-relevance-report/ethical-dilemmas-ai#:~:text=Here%20are%20some%20of%20the,lending%2C%20and%20law%20enforcement%20applications.

45. The Ethical Considerations of Artificial Intelligence | Capitol Technology University, accessed May 3, 2025, https://www.captechu.edu/blog/ethical-considerations-of-artificial-intelligence

46. Governance of artificial intelligence | Policy and Society - Oxford Academic, accessed May 3, 2025, https://academic.oup.com/policyandsociety/article/40/2/137/6509315

47. Accenture Technology Vision 2025: New Age of AI to Bring Unprecedented Autonomy to Business, accessed May 3, 2025, https://newsroom.accenture.com/news/2025/accenture-

technology-vision-2025-new-age-of-ai-to-bring-
unprecedented-autonomy-to-business

48. AI and the Future of Government: Unexpected Effects and
Critical ..., accessed May 3, 2025,
https://www.policycenter.ma/publications/ai-and-future-
government-unexpected-effects-and-critical-challenges

49. Fraud and Improper Payments: Data Quality and a Skilled
Workforce Are Essential for Unlocking the Benefits of
Artificial Intelligence - GAO, accessed May 3, 2025,
https://www.gao.gov/products/gao-25-108412

50. The Hidden Cost of Poor Data Quality: Why Your AI Initiative
Might Be Set Up for Failure, accessed May 3, 2025,
https://www.akaike.ai/resources/the-hidden-cost-of-
poor-data-quality-why-your-ai-initiative-might-be-set-up-
for-failure

51. The Surprising Reason Most AI Projects Fail – And How to
Avoid It at Your Enterprise, accessed May 3, 2025,
https://www.informatica.com/blogs/the-surprising-
reason-most-ai-projects-fail-and-how-to-avoid-it-at-your-
enterprise.html

52. Data Quality is Not Being Prioritized on AI Projects, a Trend
that 96% of U.S. Data Professionals Say Could Lead to
Widespread Crises - Qlik, accessed May 3, 2025,
https://www.qlik.com/us/news/company/press-
room/press-releases/data-quality-is-not-being-prioritized-
on-ai-projects

53. State of Georgia: AI Roadmap and Governance Framework |
Office of Artificial Intelligence, accessed May 3, 2025,
https://ai.georgia.gov/blog/2025-02-25/state-georgia-ai-
roadmap-and-governance-framework

54. Generative Artificial Intelligence and Open Data: Guidelines and Best Practices, accessed May 3, 2025, https://www.commerce.gov/news/blog/2025/01/generative-artificial-intelligence-and-open-data-guidelines-and-best-practices

55. 4 AI Use Cases for Federal Government - Interconnections - The Equinix Blog, accessed May 3, 2025, https://blog.equinix.com/blog/2025/04/10/4-ai-use-cases-for-federal-government/

56. Top 9 AI Data Governance Best Practices for Security, Compliance, and Quality, accessed May 3, 2025, https://www.pmi.org/blog/ai-data-governance-best-practices

57. AI Governance: Best Practices and Importance | Informatica, accessed May 3, 2025, https://www.informatica.com/resources/articles/ai-governance-explained.html.html.html.html.html.html.html.html.html.html.html.html.html.html.html.html.html.html

58. AI Data Governance: Definition, Best Practices & Examples - WalkMe, accessed May 3, 2025, https://www.walkme.com/blog/ai-data-governance/

59. AI Governance Best Practices - DATAVERSITY, accessed May 3, 2025, https://www.dataversity.net/ai-governance-best-practices/

60. AI Governance & Why It Is Necessary - Osano, accessed May 3, 2025, https://www.osano.com/articles/ai-governance

61. Preparing Data for AI: A Guide for Government Agencies | Casepoint, accessed May 3, 2025,

https://www.casepoint.com/blog/ai-data-preparation-for-government/

62. Understanding GDPR and CCPA in the Context of AI Systems - Signity Software Solutions, accessed May 3, 2025, https://www.signitysolutions.com/blog/understanding-gdpr-and-ccpa?hsLang=en

63. The Intersection of GDPR and AI and 6 Compliance Best Practices | Exabeam, accessed May 3, 2025, https://www.exabeam.com/explainers/gdpr-compliance/the-intersection-of-gdpr-and-ai-and-6-compliance-best-practices/

64. Managing AI to Ensure Compliance with Data Privacy Laws - Smarsh, accessed May 3, 2025, https://www.smarsh.com/blog/thought-leadership/managing-ai-to-ensure-compliance-with-data-privacy-laws

65. Highlights: The GDPR and CCPA as benchmarks for federal privacy legislation, accessed May 3, 2025, https://www.brookings.edu/articles/highlights-the-gdpr-and-ccpa-as-benchmarks-for-federal-privacy-legislation/

66. Navigating Privacy in the Age of AI: Evaluating the Adequacy of the GDPR and CCPA to Combat Data Exploitation and Deepfake Technology - NHSJS, accessed May 3, 2025, https://nhsjs.com/2024/navigating-privacy-in-the-age-of-ai-evaluating-the-adequacy-of-the-gdpr-and-ccpa-to-combat-data-exploitation-and-deepfake-technology/

67. Safeguard the Future of AI: The Core Functions of the NIST AI RMF - AuditBoard, accessed May 3, 2025, https://auditboard.com/blog/nist-ai-rmf

68. Govern - NIST AIRC - National Institute of Standards and Technology, accessed May 3, 2025, https://airc.nist.gov/airmf-resources/playbook/govern/

69. Four data and model quality challenges tied to generative AI - Deloitte, accessed May 3, 2025, https://www2.deloitte.com/us/en/insights/topics/digital-transformation/data-integrity-in-ai-engineering.html

70. How data readiness is critical to responsible AI in government | THINK Digital Partners, accessed May 3, 2025, https://www.thinkdigitalpartners.com/news/2025/04/09/how-data-readiness-is-critical-to-responsible-ai-in-government/

71. AI's Role in National Security Hinges on Data Quality | GovCIO Media & Research, accessed May 3, 2025, https://govciomedia.com/ais-role-in-national-security-hinges-on-data-quality/

72. AI Fail: 4 Root Causes & Real-life Examples in 2025 - Research AIMultiple, accessed May 3, 2025, https://research.aimultiple.com/ai-fail/

73. Concerns for AI in the Public Sector - CentralSquare, accessed May 3, 2025, https://www.centralsquare.com/resources/articles/concerns-for-ai-in-the-public-sector

74. Post #8: Into the Abyss: Examining AI Failures and Lessons Learned, accessed May 3, 2025, https://www.ethics.harvard.edu/blog/post-8-abyss-examining-ai-failures-and-lessons-learned

75. AI in government: impact to the public sector - Neudesic, accessed May 3, 2025, https://www.neudesic.com/blog/ai-in-government-public-sector-impact/

76. AWS GovCloud (US) - Amazon Web Services, accessed May 3, 2025, https://aws.amazon.com/govcloud-us/

77. Databricks Achieves FedRAMP High Authorization for AWS GovCloud - PR Newswire, accessed May 3, 2025, https://www.prnewswire.com/news-releases/databricks-achieves-fedramp-high-authorization-for-aws-govcloud-302387162.html

78. GovCloud vs Azure Government – Government Cloud Providers 101 - Anodot, accessed May 3, 2025, https://www.anodot.com/blog/aws-govcloud-vs-azure-government/

79. Could a FedRAMP rehaul usher in the US government's AI age? - FedScoop, accessed May 3, 2025, https://fedscoop.com/fedramp-government-ai-silicon-valley-cloud/

80. How GenAI Cloud Services Are Transforming Government and Military Operations, accessed May 3, 2025, https://www.ntconcepts.com/how-genai-cloud-services-are-transforming-government-and-military-operations/

81. Cloud transformation and AI benefits in the public sector - Genesys, accessed May 3, 2025, https://www.genesys.com/blog/post/cloud-transformation-and-ai-benefits-in-the-public-sector

82. Google named a Leader in The Forrester Wave™: AI Infrastructure Solutions, Q1 2024, accessed May 3, 2025,

https://cloud.google.com/resources/forrester-2024-ai-infra-wave

83. Google in The Forrester Wave AI Infrastructure Solutions, Q1 2024 | Google Cloud Blog, accessed May 3, 2025, https://cloud.google.com/blog/products/infrastructure-modernization/google-named-a-leader-in-the-forrester-wave-ai-infrastructure-solutions-q1-2024

84. High Performance Computing in AI | Deloitte US, accessed May 3, 2025, https://www2.deloitte.com/us/en/pages/consulting/articles/nvidia-alliance-high-performance-computing-in-ai.html

85. Accelerating the US Public Sector with AI - NVIDIA, accessed May 3, 2025, https://www.nvidia.com/en-us/industries/public-sector/

86. GPU Nodes for AI, ML and HPC - Nscale, accessed May 3, 2025, https://www.nscale.com/product/gpu-nodes

87. Advanced HPC & AI Solutions for Research Computing - Cambridge Computer, accessed May 3, 2025, https://www.cambridgecomputer.com/research-computing/

88. Compute servers | Dell Validated Design for Government HPC, Artificial Intelligence, and Data Analytics: AI Inferencing Option, accessed May 3, 2025, https://infohub.delltechnologies.com/l/dell-validated-design-for-government-hpc-artificial-intelligence-and-data-analytics-ai-inferencing-option-1/compute-servers-31/

89. Dell's AI Infrastructure Makes Waves in Forrester Report, accessed May 3, 2025, https://www.dell.com/en-

us/blog/dells-ai-infrastructure-makes-waves-in-forrester-report/

90. Advancing United States Leadership in Artificial Intelligence Infrastructure - Federal Register, accessed May 3, 2025, https://www.federalregister.gov/documents/2025/01/17/2025-01395/advancing-united-states-leadership-in-artificial-intelligence-infrastructure

91. Request for Information on Artificial Intelligence Infrastructure on DOE Lands, accessed May 3, 2025, https://www.federalregister.gov/documents/2025/04/07/2025-05936/request-for-information-on-artificial-intelligence-infrastructure-on-doe-lands

92. The Roles of Edge Computing, AI & 5G in DOD Tactical Ops - GovCon Wire, accessed May 3, 2025, https://www.govconwire.com/2025/01/dod-edge-computing-ai-5g-research-development/

93. AI in Government: A Strategic Framework for Digital Transformation - REI Systems, accessed May 3, 2025, https://www.reisystems.com/ai-in-government-a-strategic-framework-for-digital-transformation/

94. Using AI in Local Government: 10 Use Cases - Oracle, accessed May 3, 2025, https://www.oracle.com/artificial-intelligence/ai-local-government/

95. Understanding AI in government: Applications, use cases, and implementation | Elastic Blog, accessed May 3, 2025, https://www.elastic.co/blog/ai-government

96. VAST Data Platform: AI-Powered Discovery Engine, accessed May 3, 2025, https://www.vastdata.com/platform/overview

97. Use Cases of AI in Government | Snowflake, accessed May 3, 2025, https://www.snowflake.com/trending/use-cases-ai-government/

98. I am interested in government applications of AI. What are some useful applications and how were they developed? - Career Village, accessed May 3, 2025, https://www.careervillage.org/questions/1014598/i-am-interested-in-government-applications-of-ai-what-are-some-useful-applications-and-how-were-they-developed

99. Report Artificial Intelligence and Law Enforcement: The Federal and State Landscape, accessed May 3, 2025, https://www.ncsl.org/civil-and-criminal-justice/artificial-intelligence-and-law-enforcement-the-federal-and-state-landscape

100. Big Data Analytics in Government: Benefits & Uses - One Federal Solution, accessed May 3, 2025, https://www.onefederalsolution.com/big-data-analytics-in-the-government-sector/

101. Improving Government Case Management with AI: 6 Use Cases - Appian, accessed May 3, 2025, https://appian.com/blog/acp/public-sector/ai-use-cases-government-case-management

102. AI in Government: How Government CIOs Can Capture AI Potential - Gartner, accessed May 3, 2025, https://www.gartner.com/en/information-technology/topics/ai-in-government

103. Top 10 Applications of Artificial Intelligence in Government Services | Tars Blog, accessed May 3, 2025, https://hellotars.com/blog/top-10-applications-of-artificial-intelligence-in-government-services

104. Deloitte AI Institute for Government, accessed May 3, 2025, https://www2.deloitte.com/us/en/pages/public-sector/articles/artificial-intelligence-government-sector.html

105. Generative AI Makes Information Accessible | Deloitte US, accessed May 3, 2025, https://www2.deloitte.com/us/en/pages/public-sector/articles/ai-in-government-case-stories.html

106. Cybersecurity and Infrastructure Security Agency – AI Use Cases, accessed May 3, 2025, https://www.dhs.gov/ai/use-case-inventory/cisa

107. Role of NLP in the Public Sector - Cogent Infotech, accessed May 3, 2025, https://www.cogentinfo.com/resources/nlp-in-the-public-sector

108. Gen AI in Government: Opportunities, Challenges and Risks - Cerium Networks, accessed May 3, 2025, https://ceriumnetworks.com/gen-ai-in-government-opportunities-challenges-and-risks/

109. Natural Language Processing Examples in Government Data | Deloitte Insights, accessed May 3, 2025, https://www2.deloitte.com/us/en/insights/focus/cognitive-technologies/natural-language-processing-examples-in-government-data.html

110. What Is NLP (Natural Language Processing)? - IBM, accessed May 3, 2025, https://www.ibm.com/think/topics/natural-language-processing

111. Top 30+ NLP Use Cases in 2025 with Real-life Examples - Research AIMultiple, accessed May 3, 2025, https://research.aimultiple.com/nlp-use-cases/

112. AI for Government: ChatGPT in the Public Sector [With Prompts!] - OpenGov, accessed May 3, 2025, https://opengov.com/article/ai-for-government/

113. How Law Enforcement Uses AI for Public Safety & Privacy - Sighthound Redactor, accessed May 3, 2025, https://www.redactor.com/blog/law-enforcement-leveraging-computer-vision-for-safety-and-privacy

114. Computer Vision Use Cases In Government Sector - Cogent Infotech, accessed May 3, 2025, https://www.cogentinfo.com/resources/computer-vision-use-cases-in-government-sector

115. Law Enforcement on the AI Frontier: Seizing the Potential Requires Strong Fundamentals, accessed May 3, 2025, https://www.saic.com/features/data-and-ai/law-enforcement-on-the-AI-frontier

116. How AI can enable public surveillance - Brookings Institution, accessed May 3, 2025, https://www.brookings.edu/articles/how-ai-can-enable-public-surveillance/

117. Computer Vision: How Federal Government Can Use AI To Advance Beyond Image Processing - Cogent Infotech, accessed May 3, 2025, https://www.cogentinfo.com/resources/computer-vision-how-feds-can-use-ai-to-advance-beyond-image-processing

118. Improve Government Operations with Computer Vision - Roboflow, accessed May 3, 2025, https://roboflow.com/industries/government

119. How Computer Vision Is Helping Agencies See Their Mission Objectives More Clearly, accessed May 3, 2025, https://fedtechmagazine.com/article/2021/02/how-computer-vision-helping-agencies-see-their-mission-objectives-more-clearly

120. 7 Practical Applications of AI in Government - V7 Labs, accessed May 3, 2025, https://www.v7labs.com/blog/ai-in-government

121. Generative AI for the Public Sector: From Opportunities to Value - Foreign Policy, accessed May 3, 2025, https://sponsored.foreignpolicy.com/bcg/generative-ai-for-the-public-sector-from-opportunities-to-value/

122. Gen AI for Government: Benefits, Risks and Implementation Process - Digital Divide Data, accessed May 3, 2025, https://www.digitaldividedata.com/blog/gen-ai-for-government

123. The Role and Use of AI In Local Government - CivicPlus, accessed May 3, 2025, https://www.civicplus.com/blog/cxp/role-use-ai-local-government/

124. Guiding Principles on Government Use of Surveillance Technologies, accessed May 3, 2025, https://freedomonlinecoalition.com/guiding-principles-on-government-use-of-surveillance-technologies/

125. Governance of Generative AI | Policy and Society - Oxford Academic, accessed May 3, 2025,

https://academic.oup.com/policyandsociety/article/44/1/1/7997395

126. AI and the Future of Democracy: Challenges and Opportunities | FSI - Stanford University, accessed May 3, 2025, https://fsi.stanford.edu/events/ai-and-future-democracy-challenges-and-opportunities

127. Data and AI Driven solutions for Federal Government - Databricks, accessed May 3, 2025, https://www.databricks.com/solutions/industries/federal-government

128. AI Roadmap: What It Is and How to Build One - Gartner, accessed May 3, 2025, https://www.gartner.com/en/articles/ai-roadmap

129. Preparing Federal Agency Infrastructure for AI Using a 3-Year Strategic Plan - GovLoop, accessed May 3, 2025, https://www.govloop.com/community/blog/preparing-federal-agency-infrastructure-for-ai-using-a-3-year-strategic-plan/

130. Digital Twins: Transforming Government Operations with Interoperability, accessed May 3, 2025, https://spaceproject.govexec.com/ideas/2024/12/digital-twins-transforming-government-operations-interoperability/401481/

131. M-25-22-Driving-Efficient-Acquisition-of-Artificial-Intelligence-in-Government.pdf - The White House, accessed May 3, 2025, https://www.whitehouse.gov/wp-content/uploads/2025/02/M-25-22-Driving-Efficient-Acquisition-of-Artificial-Intelligence-in-Government.pdf

132. Trump Administration Revamps Guidance on Federal Use and Procurement of AI, accessed May 3, 2025,

https://www.wiley.law/alert-Trump-Administration-Revamps-Guidance-on-Federal-Use-and-Procurement-of-AI

133. Using AI to Write Police Reports - COPS Office, accessed May 3, 2025, https://cops.usdoj.gov/html/dispatch/01-2025/ai_reports.html

134. Using AI & Analytics to Enhance Law Enforcement Surveillance - Critical Tech Solutions, accessed May 3, 2025, https://www.criticalts.com/articles/how-ai-analytics-are-revolutionizing-law-enforcement-surveillance/

135. Police use of AI: A Force for good or a public threat? - Eviden, accessed May 3, 2025, https://eviden.com/insights/blogs/police-use-of-ai-a-force-for-good-or-a-public-threat/

136. Mitigating Bias in AI: How Companies Can Build Fairer AI Systems - FullStack Labs, accessed May 3, 2025, https://www.fullstack.com/labs/resources/blog/mitigating-bias-in-ai-how-to-build-fairer-ai

137. Accountable Artificial Intelligence: Holding Algorithms to Account - PMC - PubMed Central, accessed May 3, 2025, https://pmc.ncbi.nlm.nih.gov/articles/PMC8518786/

138. NLP in the Public Sector - Cogent Infotech, accessed May 3, 2025, https://www.cogentinfo.com/resources/nlp-examples-in-the-public-sector

139. 10 Ways the US Government is Using AI [2025] - DigitalDefynd, accessed May 3, 2025, https://digitaldefynd.com/IQ/ways-the-us-government-using-ai/

140. Ensuring AI Is Used Responsibly - Homeland Security, accessed May 3, 2025, https://www.dhs.gov/ai/ensuring-ai-is-used-responsibly

141. 7 ways AI could restore trust in public services - The World Economic Forum, accessed May 3, 2025, https://www.weforum.org/stories/2021/01/ai-trust-public-services/

142. AI Transforming UK Government: Boost Efficiency & Innovation - - Farmonaut, accessed May 3, 2025, https://farmonaut.com/united-kingdom/revolutionizing-public-services-how-ai-is-transforming-uk-government-efficiency-and-innovation

143. Singapore introduces three new AI governance initiatives - GovInsider, accessed May 3, 2025, https://govinsider.asia/intl-en/article/singapore-introduces-three-new-ai-governance-initiatives

144. Estonia's groundbreaking national initiative: AI Leap programme to bring AI tools to all schools, accessed May 3, 2025, https://e-estonia.com/estonia-announces-a-groundbreaking-national-initiative-ai-leap-programme-to-bring-ai-tools-to-all-schools/

145. AI in Government that Actually Works | IE Insights, accessed May 3, 2025, https://www.ie.edu/insights/articles/ai-systems-in-public-administration/

146. Transforming Public Sector With AI: Opportunities and Challenges - StateTech Magazine, accessed May 3, 2025, https://statetechmagazine.com/article/2025/02/transforming-public-sector-ai-opportunities-and-challenges

147. AI business case: Reduce cost and optimize resources - Insights2Action - Deloitte, accessed May 3, 2025, https://action.deloitte.com/insight/3246/ai-business-case-reduce-cost-and-optimize-resources

148. Scaling AI in Public Sector Decision-Making - Avero Advisors, accessed May 3, 2025, https://averoadvisors.com/scaling-ai-in-public-sector-decision-making/

149. Government Agencies and RPA: Key Tips for Choosing Wisely! - REI Systems, accessed May 3, 2025, https://www.reisystems.com/government-agencies-and-rpa-key-tips-for-choosing-wisely/

150. AI in government: AI law, use cases, and challenges - Pluralsight, accessed May 3, 2025, https://www.pluralsight.com/resources/blog/ai-and-data/ai-government-public-sector

151. Why Have Governments Been Slow to Adopt AI? - Technology Magazine, accessed May 3, 2025, https://technologymagazine.com/ai-and-machine-learning/why-have-governments-been-slow-to-adopt-ai

152. Making the case for Artificial Intelligence (AI) in Transforming Public Services, accessed May 3, 2025, https://wwps.microsoft.com/wp-content/uploads/2025/02/Making-the-case-for-AI-in-Public-Services-ROI-evaluation.pdf

153. The Trends, Challenges And Future Of AI In E-Governance - Forbes, accessed May 3, 2025, https://www.forbes.com/councils/forbestechcouncil/2025/05/02/the-trends-challenges-and-future-of-ai-in-e-governance/

154. Using AI to Simulate Congress - It's a Whole New World | Political Affairs - Ozean Media, accessed May 3, 2025, https://ozeanmedia.com/political-research/using-ai-to-simulate-congress-its-a-whole-new-world/

155. Explainable AI in Government: Transparency, Trust, and Traceability | The AI Journal, accessed May 3, 2025, https://aijourn.com/explainable-ai-in-government-transparency-trust-and-traceability/

156. Full article: Holding AI-Based Systems Accountable in the Public Sector: A Systematic Review - Taylor & Francis Online, accessed May 3, 2025, https://www.tandfonline.com/doi/full/10.1080/15309576.2025.2469784?af=R

157. The Government and Public Services AI Dossier - Deloitte, accessed May 3, 2025, https://www2.deloitte.com/us/en/pages/consulting/articles/ai-dossier-government-public-services.html

158. Accelerating Artificial Intelligence (AI) in the Public Sector - - GrantSolutions, accessed May 3, 2025, https://home.grantsolutions.gov/home/event-recap/accelerating-artificial-intelligence-ai-in-the-public-sector/

159. AI Governance Frameworks: Guide to Ethical AI Implementation - Consilien, accessed May 3, 2025, https://www.consilien.com/news/ai-governance-frameworks-guide-to-ethical-ai-implementation

160. AI Governance Frameworks: Guide to Ethical AI Implementation - Consilien, accessed May 3, 2025, https://consilien.com/news/ai-governance-frameworks-guide-to-ethical-ai-implementation

161. Brief Artificial Intelligence in Government: The Federal and State Landscape, accessed May 3, 2025, https://www.ncsl.org/technology-and-communication/artificial-intelligence-in-government-the-federal-and-state-landscape

162. U.S. Joins with OECD in Adopting Global AI Principles, accessed May 3, 2025, https://www.ntia.gov/blog/us-joins-oecd-adopting-global-ai-principles

163. Artificial intelligence - OECD, accessed May 3, 2025, https://www.oecd.org/en/topics/artificial-intelligence.html

164. How countries are implementing the OECD Principles for Trustworthy AI, accessed May 3, 2025, https://oecd.ai/en/wonk/national-policies-2

165. AI Governance Frameworks - Data Strategy Professionals, accessed May 3, 2025, https://www.datastrategypros.com/resources/aigfc/frameworks

166. April 3, 2025 M-25-21 MEMORANDUM FOR THE HEADS OF EXECUTIVE DEPARTMENTS AND AGENCIES FROM: R~ssell T. Vought \\ 1 \ Director \J - The White House, accessed May 3, 2025, https://www.whitehouse.gov/wp-content/uploads/2025/02/M-25-21-Accelerating-Federal-Use-of-AI-through-Innovation-Governance-and-Public-Trust.pdf

167. OMB Issues First Trump 2.0-Era Requirements for AI Use and Procurement by Federal Agencies | Inside Government Contracts, accessed May 3, 2025, https://www.insidegovernmentcontracts.com/2025/04/o

mb-issues-first-trump-2-0-era-requirements-for-ai-use-and-procurement-by-federal-agencies/

168. Artificial Intelligence: GAO's Work to Leverage Technology and Ensure Responsible Use, accessed May 3, 2025, https://www.gao.gov/products/gao-24-107237

169. Artificial Intelligence: Agencies Have Begun Implementation but Need to Complete Key Requirements - GAO, accessed May 3, 2025, https://www.gao.gov/products/gao-24-105980

170. General Services Administration: Data Ethics Framework (2020) - IAPP, accessed May 3, 2025, https://iapp.org/resources/article/general-services-administration-data-ethics-framework-2020/

171. What is AI transparency? A comprehensive guide - Zendesk, accessed May 3, 2025, https://www.zendesk.com/blog/ai-transparency/

172. What Does Transparency Really Mean in the Context of AI Governance? - OCEG, accessed May 3, 2025, https://www.oceg.org/what-does-transparency-really-mean-in-the-context-of-ai-governance/

173. What Is Explainable AI (XAI)? - Palo Alto Networks, accessed May 3, 2025, https://www.paloaltonetworks.com/cyberpedia/explainable-ai

174. Privacy and responsible AI - IAPP, accessed May 3, 2025, https://iapp.org/news/a/privacy-and-responsible-ai

175. Full article: AI Ethics: Integrating Transparency, Fairness, and Privacy in AI Development, accessed May 3, 2025,

https://www.tandfonline.com/doi/full/10.1080/08839514.2025.2463722

176. Ethical Considerations of AI | What Purpose do Fairness Measures Serve in AI? | Lumenalta, accessed May 3, 2025, https://lumenalta.com/insights/ethical-considerations-of-ai

177. How to Mitigate Bias in AI Systems Through AI Governance - Holistic AI, accessed May 3, 2025, https://www.holisticai.com/blog/mitigate-bias-ai-systems-governance

178. AI Bias: Types, Examples & 6 Debiasing Strategies - Dialzara, accessed May 3, 2025, https://dialzara.com/blog/ai-bias-types-examples-and-6-debiasing-strategies/

179. Cyber Threats and Advisories | Cybersecurity and Infrastructure Security Agency CISA, accessed May 3, 2025, https://www.cisa.gov/topics/cyber-threats-and-advisories

180. ENISA space threat landscape report highlights cybersecurity gaps in commercial satellites, urges enhanced defense - Industrial Cyber, accessed May 3, 2025, https://industrialcyber.co/vulnerabilities/enisa-space-threat-landscape-report-highlights-cybersecurity-gaps-in-commercial-satellites-urges-enhanced-defense/

181. Artificial Intelligence Ethics Framework for the Intelligence Community - INTEL.gov, accessed May 3, 2025, https://www.intelligence.gov/artificial-intelligence-ethics-framework-for-the-intelligence-community

182. Bias recognition and mitigation strategies in artificial intelligence healthcare applications - PMC - PubMed

Central, accessed May 3, 2025,
https://pmc.ncbi.nlm.nih.gov/articles/PMC11897215/

183. ALGORITHMIC ACCOUNTABILITY: The Need for a New
Approach to Transparency and Accountability When
Government Functions Are Perfor - Yale Law School,
accessed May 3, 2025,
https://law.yale.edu/sites/default/files/area/center/mfia
/document/algorithmic_accountability_report.pdf

184. "Hey SyRI, tell me about algorithmic accountability":
Lessons from a landmark case | Data & Policy | Cambridge
Core, accessed May 3, 2025,
https://www.cambridge.org/core/journals/data-and-
policy/article/hey-syri-tell-me-about-algorithmic-
accountability-lessons-from-a-landmark-
case/22A3086554B0486BB4BBAF2D5A33A3D0

185. 10 Real AI Bias Examples & Mitigation Guide -
Crescendo.ai, accessed May 3, 2025,
https://www.crescendo.ai/blog/ai-bias-examples-
mitigation-guide

186. AI Accountability Starts with Government Transparency |
TechPolicy.Press, accessed May 3, 2025,
https://www.techpolicy.press/ai-accountability-starts-
with-government-transparency/

187. Algorithmic accountability for the public sector - Open
Government Partnership, accessed May 3, 2025,
https://www.opengovpartnership.org/wp-
content/uploads/2021/08/algorithmic-accountability-
public-sector.pdf

188. DHS Unveils Generative AI Public Sector Playbook |
Homeland Security, accessed May 3, 2025,

https://www.dhs.gov/archive/news/2025/01/07/dhs-unveils-generative-ai-public-sector-playbook

189. What the public thinks about AI and the implications for governance - Brookings Institution, accessed May 3, 2025, https://www.brookings.edu/articles/what-the-public-thinks-about-ai-and-the-implications-for-governance/

190. AI and Government Agencies: Current Trends and Future Prospects - APHSA, accessed May 3, 2025, https://aphsa.org/resources/ai-in-government/

191. Ethical and Responsible AI Adoption in Government - REI Systems, accessed May 3, 2025, https://www.reisystems.com/roadmap-to-transformation-the-next-generation-of-government-operations-with-ethical-and-responsible-ai-adoption/

192. ENISA reports that skills shortage and unpatched systems are among top cyber threats for 2030, accessed May 3, 2025, https://industrialcyber.co/reports/enisa-reports-that-skills-shortage-and-unpatched-systems-are-among-top-cyber-threats-for-2030/

193. ENISA: Home, accessed May 3, 2025, https://www.enisa.europa.eu/

194. Navigating CMMC Compliance: Proactive IT Strategies for Civil Engineering in 2025, accessed May 3, 2025, https://govdesignhub.com/2025/02/13/navigating-cmmc-compliance-proactive-it-strategies-for-civil-engineering-in-2025/

195. 2025 CMMC Security Guide - Concentric AI, accessed May 3, 2025, https://concentric.ai/a-guide-to-cmmc-compliance/

196. CMMC - Compliance | Google Cloud, accessed May 3, 2025, https://cloud.google.com/security/compliance/cmmc

197. CMMC Compliance Requirements: A Complete Guide - Legit Security, accessed May 3, 2025, https://www.legitsecurity.com/blog/cmmc-compliance-requirements

198. What Is CMMC Compliance? An Overview of the DoD CSF - AuditBoard, accessed May 3, 2025, https://auditboard.com/blog/what-is-the-cmmc-framework

199. A Government Roadmap On How To Navigate The AI Revolution - Oliver Wyman, accessed May 3, 2025, https://www.oliverwyman.com/our-expertise/insights/2025/jan/government-roadmap-how-to-navigate-ai-revolution.html

200. Strategic Steps: Generative AI Adoption in the Public Sector - OGx Consulting, accessed May 3, 2025, https://www.weareogx.com/ai-roadmap/

201. CortexAI for Government™: Next Generation of AI Government Solutions | Deloitte US, accessed May 3, 2025, https://www2.deloitte.com/us/en/pages/consulting/topics/ai-government-solutions.html

202. State and Local Government AI Roadmap, accessed May 3, 2025, https://www.csg.org/wp-content/uploads/sites/7/2024/12/Microsoft-AI-Government-Roadmap.pdf

203. Roadmap: The Future of Digital Government Strategy - Gartner, accessed May 3, 2025,

https://www.gartner.com/en/publications/transitioning-to-digital-government-roadmap

204. United States Department of Agriculture Fiscal Year 2025–2026 AI Strategy - USDA, accessed May 3, 2025, https://www.usda.gov/sites/default/files/documents/fy-2025-2026-usda-ai-strategy.pdf

205. Enhancing Public Sector: Innovative Cutting-Edge Gov Tech Strategies - Number Analytics, accessed May 3, 2025, https://www.numberanalytics.com/blog/enhancing-public-sector-cutting-edge-gov-tech-strategies

206. Driving AI Change and Innovation: Revolutionizing Public Sector Practices, accessed May 3, 2025, https://www.numberanalytics.com/blog/driving-ai-change-public-sector

207. Harnessing AI and Machine Learning for Government Workforce Development - ATD, accessed May 3, 2025, https://www.td.org/content/atd-blog/harnessing-ai-and-machine-learning-for-government-workforce-development?__queryID=fcba992856b84f340355ee5624f5f8a6&objectID=SxYx3xvB0upPDkmSEysfA&__position=1&index=atd_composable_prod_en-US_newest

208. AI Government Leadership Program - Partnership for Public Service, accessed May 3, 2025, https://ourpublicservice.org/course/ai-government-leadership-program/

209. Skilling at Scale: How strategic partnerships are transforming the way public sector organizations deliver skilling, accessed May 3, 2025, https://wwps.microsoft.com/blog/skilling-partnerships

210. AI Workforce Development | Info-Tech Research Group, accessed May 3, 2025, https://www.infotech.com/it-leadership-training/ai-workforce-development

211. AI Training Series for Government Employees | GSA, accessed May 3, 2025, https://coe.gsa.gov/communities/AITraining.html

212. AI in Government and Public Sector: The Need for Certified Professionals - PECB, accessed May 3, 2025, https://pecb.com/article/ai-in-government-and-public-sector-the-need-for-certified-professionals

213. How we work | United States Digital Service, accessed May 3, 2025, https://www.usds.gov/how-we-work

214. Generative AI: Reinventing work for public service organizations - Accenture, accessed May 3, 2025, https://www.accenture.com/us-en/blogs/public-service/generative-ai-reinventing-work-public-service

215. The state of AI: How organizations are rewiring to capture value - McKinsey & Company, accessed May 3, 2025, https://www.mckinsey.com/capabilities/quantumblack/our-insights/the-state-of-ai

216. Accenture: Transforming Public Service, accessed May 3, 2025, https://www.acntransformingpublicservice.com/

217. The UK Government Is Ready To Embrace AI, But Without Trust, It Risks Disaster - Forrester, accessed May 3, 2025, https://www.forrester.com/blogs/the-uk-government-is-ready-to-embrace-ai-but-without-trust-it-risks-disaster/

218. Big Five Consulting: Betting Billions on AI Partnerships by Virtasant, accessed May 3, 2025,

https://www.virtasant.com/ai-today/big-five-consulting-betting-billions-on-ai-partnerships

219. Public Sector Consulting and Strategy | BCG, accessed May 3, 2025, https://www.bcg.com/industries/public-sector/overview

220. Generative AI for the Public Sector: The Journey to Scale, accessed May 3, 2025, https://www.bcg.com/publications/2024/gen-ai-journey-to-scale-in-government

221. Superagency in the workplace: Empowering people to unlock AI's full potential - McKinsey & Company, accessed May 3, 2025, https://www.mckinsey.com/capabilities/mckinsey-digital/our-insights/superagency-in-the-workplace-empowering-people-to-unlock-ais-full-potential-at-work

222. The Top 20 Best AI Consultant Firms and Why They Rank - Redress Compliance, accessed May 3, 2025, https://redresscompliance.com/the-top-20-best-ai-consultant-firms-and-why-they-rank/

223. Innovation, Governance, and Public Trust: The US Office of Management and Budget (OMB) Issues Guidance on AI - The Scholarly Kitchen, accessed May 3, 2025, https://scholarlykitchen.sspnet.org/2025/04/28/innovation-governance-and-public-trust-the-us-office-of-management-and-budget-omb-issues-guidance-on-ai/

224. Technical Contributions to AI Governance | NIST, accessed May 3, 2025, https://www.nist.gov/artificial-intelligence/technical-contributions-ai-governance

225. Digital Development in 2025: Ten Moments to Watch, accessed May 3, 2025,

https://www.undp.org/digital/blog/digital-development-2025-ten-moments-watch

226. The World Bank showcases new white paper on DPI as it seeks to accelerate digital transformation | Biometric Update, accessed May 3, 2025, https://www.biometricupdate.com/202503/the-world-bank-showcases-new-white-paper-on-dpi-as-it-seeks-to-accelerate-digital-transformation

227. World Bank Group (WBG) - AI for Good - ITU, accessed May 3, 2025, https://aiforgood.itu.int/about-us/un-ai-actions/wbg/

228. The AI governance balancing act: Navigating opportunities and risks - World Bank Blogs, accessed May 3, 2025, https://blogs.worldbank.org/en/digital-development/the-ai-governance-balancing-act--navigating-opportunities-and-ri

229. Governing with Artificial Intelligence - OECD, accessed May 3, 2025, https://www.oecd.org/en/publications/governing-with-artificial-intelligence_26324bc2-en.html

230. Examining AI Safety as a Global Public Good: Implications, Challenges, and Research Priorities | Carnegie Endowment for International Peace, accessed May 3, 2025, https://carnegieendowment.org/research/2025/03/examining-ai-safety-as-a-global-public-good-implications-challenges-and-research-priorities?lang=en

231. Public AI infrastructure: What is it, do we need it and will it ever be built? A media leader explains, accessed May 3, 2025, https://www.weforum.org/stories/2025/02/public-ai-infrastructure-a-media-leader-explains/

232. Analyzing the Long-Term Societal Impact of Artificial Intelligence Integration in Public Sector Policy and Governance Systems - ijcsitr, accessed May 3, 2025, https://ijcsitr.com/index.php/home/article/view/IJCSITR_2025_06_03_001

233. AI Societal Impact Assessment: Measuring the Broader Effects of AI Initiatives - AIGN, accessed May 3, 2025, https://aign.global/ai-governance-consulting/patrick-upmann/ai-societal-impact-assessment-measuring-the-broader-effects-of-ai-initiatives/

234. Governing AI for the Future of Humanity - Stimson Center, accessed May 3, 2025, https://www.stimson.org/2025/governing-ai-for-the-future-of-humanity/

235. Strategic Foresight and Artificial Intelligence - TRENDS Research & Advisory, accessed May 3, 2025, https://trendsresearch.org/podcast/strategic-foresight-and-artificial-intelligence/

236. Applying History to Inform Anticipatory AI Governance - RAND, accessed May 3, 2025, https://www.rand.org/pubs/conf_proceedings/CFA3591-1.html

237. Predictions for AI's next 20 years by the US public and AI experts | Pew Research Center, accessed May 3, 2025, https://www.pewresearch.org/internet/2025/04/03/public-and-expert-predictions-for-ais-next-20-years/

238. How AI can be detrimental to our social fabric | Infosys BPM, accessed May 3, 2025, https://www.infosysbpm.com/blogs/business-

transformation/how-ai-can-be-detrimental-to-our-social-fabric.html

239. The impact of artificial intelligence on human society and bioethics - PMC, accessed May 3, 2025, https://pmc.ncbi.nlm.nih.gov/articles/PMC7605294/

240. Artificial intelligence and economic and financial policymaking A high-level panel of experts' report to the G7, accessed May 3, 2025, https://www.dt.mef.gov.it/export/sites/sitodt/modules/documenti_it/HLPE-Report-on-AI.pdf

241. Artificial Intelligence: Generative AI's Environmental and Human Effects | U.S. GAO, accessed May 3, 2025, https://www.gao.gov/products/gao-25-107172

242. Full article: Artificial intelligence and democracy: pathway to progress or decline?, accessed May 3, 2025, https://www.tandfonline.com/doi/full/10.1080/19331681.2025.2473994

243. An Agenda to Strengthen U.S. Democracy in the Age of AI | Brennan Center for Justice, accessed May 3, 2025, https://www.brennancenter.org/our-work/policy-solutions/agenda-strengthen-us-democracy-age-ai

244. A technical AI government agency plays a vital role in advancing AI innovation and trustworthiness - Brookings Institution, accessed May 3, 2025, https://www.brookings.edu/articles/a-technical-ai-government-agency-plays-a-vital-role-in-advancing-ai-innovation-and-trustworthiness/

245. Sustaining America's technology preeminence - Deloitte, accessed May 3, 2025, https://www2.deloitte.com/us/en/insights/industry/publi

c-sector/america-pole-position-future-technology-predictions.html

246. Deloitte Global's 2025 Predictions Report: Generative AI: Paving the Way for a transformative future in Technology, Media, and Telecommunications, accessed May 3, 2025, https://www.deloitte.com/global/en/about/press-room/deloitte-globals-2025-predictions-report.html

247. Artificial Intelligence (AI) and Strategic Foresight - Inspenet, accessed May 3, 2025, https://inspenet.com/en/articulo/impact-of-ai-on-strategic-foresight/

248. Digital twins – dynamic models that respond to real-time data - POST Parliament, accessed May 3, 2025, https://post.parliament.uk/digital-twins-dynamic-models-that-respond-to-real-time-data/

249. Digital Twin - Government Acquisitions Inc., accessed May 3, 2025, https://gov-acq.com/gai-solutions/digital-twin/

250. Three Ways AI-Powered Digital Twins Can Improve Government Services, accessed May 3, 2025, https://www.businessofgovernment.org/blog/three-ways-ai-powered-digital-twins-can-improve-government-services

251. AI expert Andy Lin discusses the future of digital twins, accessed May 3, 2025, https://phhp.ufl.edu/2024/11/25/ai-expert-andy-lin-discusses-the-future-of-digital-twins/

252. CMV: Artificial Intelligence would be the best form of government : r/changemyview - Reddit, accessed May 3, 2025,

https://www.reddit.com/r/changemyview/comments/res iba/cmv_artificial_intelligence_would_be_the_best/

253. Would you live under an AI government? : r/singularity - Reddit, accessed May 3, 2025, https://www.reddit.com/r/singularity/comments/13j8ndl /would_you_live_under_an_ai_government/

254. The Future of Politics in the Age of AI - RTS Labs, accessed May 3, 2025, https://rtslabs.com/future-of-politics-in-the-age-of-ai

255. The future of AI and democracy | Stanford University School of Engineering, accessed May 3, 2025, https://engineering.stanford.edu/news/future-ai-and-democracy

256. AI can strengthen U.S. democracy—and weaken it - Brookings Institution, accessed May 3, 2025, https://www.brookings.edu/articles/ai-can-strengthen-u-s-democracy-and-weaken-it/

257. Ensuring a Whole-of-Government Approach to Delivering UK AI Opportunities, accessed May 3, 2025, https://institute.global/insights/tech-and-digitalisation/ensuring-a-whole-of-government-approach-to-delivering-uk-ai-opportunities

www.ingramcontent.com/pod-product-compliance
Lightning Source LLC
LaVergne TN
LVHW051626250725
817094LV00009B/124